GUITAR *signature licks*

VOLUME 2

Jimi Hendrix

BY CHAD JOHNSON

Cover Photo by Peter Amft

ISBN 0-634-07772-4

EXPERIENCE
HENDRIX™

EXCLUSIVELY DISTRIBUTED BY

HAL•LEONARD®
CORPORATION

7777 W. BLUEMOUND RD. P.O. BOX 13819 MILWAUKEE, WI 53213

Visit Hal Leonard Online at
www.halleonard.com

CONTENTS

INTRODUCTION

There have certainly been many musical acts that have changed the face of pop music forever: Elvis, the Beatles, Led Zeppelin, etc. However, most bands that affect the musical world in this way usually enjoy fairly long recording careers of a decade or more. Jimi Hendrix turned the music world (let alone the guitar world!) upside down, and he did it with a recording career that lasted just over three years.

In this second volume of *Jimi Hendrix Signature Licks*, we'll explore twelve more classics from the Hendrix catalog. We'll study each one in depth, focusing on the tone, guitar techniques, production techniques, compositional devices, and all the other aspects that made Hendrix the undeniable musical force that he was. From the delicate "Angel" to the mellow otherworldliness of "Third Stone from the Sun" and the magical virtuosic display of "Machine Gun," we'll get a glimpse into all facets of Jimi's unbridled guitar genius.

All of the guitar parts are represented on the accompanying recording, and the difficult guitar parts are slowed down and isolated for closer examination. While every effort has been made to duplicate the sounds heard on the original recordings, please remember that there is only one Hendrix; in order to truly experience his music you need to listen to his definitive versions. Now let's get on it with it, and prepare to have your guitar-playing mind blown...

THE RECORDING

Doug Boduch:	guitar
Warren Wiegratz:	keyboards
Tom McGirr:	bass
Scott Schroedl:	drums

Recorded at The Dream Factory, Madison, WI

Produced by Jake Johnson

Follow the audio icons (♦) in the book to keep your spot on the CD. The track icons are placed after the figure numbers at the top of each figure. When more than one icon appears after a figure, the first track listed is a recording of the figure in full. All other track numbers listed are notable guitar parts played more slowly.

ALL ALONG THE WATCHTOWER

(*Electric Ladyland*, 1968)

Words and Music by Bob Dylan

Though many artists throughout the years have covered this classic Bob Dylan song, Hendrix's rendition is without a doubt the most popular. Released on his masterpiece *Electric Ladyland* album, Hendrix treats the song to a beautiful arrangement combining 12-string acoustics with his classic riff style on clean-tone electric.

Figure 1—Intro

One of the most rhythmically misinterpreted riffs in history, "Watchtower" opens with a syncopated chordal figure played by two 12-string acoustics (arranged for one guitar, Gtr. 1) that outlines the basic C#m–B–A–B (i–bVII–bVI–bVII) progression that will continue throughout the rest of the song. The fact that the chord changes are anticipated by an eighth note each time, coupled with the drums' offbeat accents, results in an ambiguous sense of beat that's not resolved until the proper entrance of the full band in measure 5.

At that point, Jimi kicks off his brief, four-measure intro solo using a beautiful, slightly distorted tone (Gtr. 2). Though mostly drawing from the C# minor pentatonic scale (C#–E–F#–G#–B) in ninth position, there are a few notable exceptions. He opens the solo in the "extended box" position (sometimes referred to as the "B.B. King box") in twelfth position with a tonic C# note bent a whole step to the colorful 9th (D#). In measure 8, Hendrix executes a quick hammer-on/pull-off figure on beat 1 involving G# and A#. It's unclear as to whether this A# is erroneous (it's actually occurring over an A chord!), but the result is a unique sound that only adds additional character to the short, succinct intro statement.

Notice the expressive devices used throughout the solo: pre-bends (measures 5 and 7), slides (measures 5 and 6), and Hendrix's trademark beautiful vibrato throughout. Also note the imitative rhythmic phrasing that Hendrix employs.

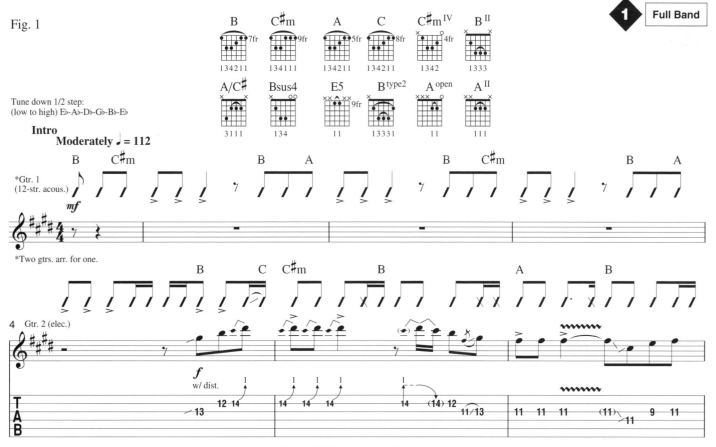

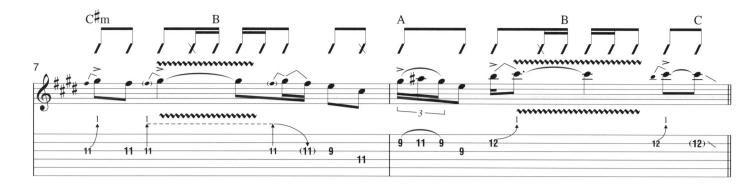

Figure 2—Verse

For the verse, Gtr. 1 streamlines its approach to mostly sustained half-note chords. Beneath this, Gtr. 2 riffs through the chord progression in classic Jimi style, combining the arpeggiation of chords with R&B-style hammer-pull figures. This chordal approach has become synonymous with Hendrix over the years and is now usually referred to as the "Hendrix Style" by most guitarists. Notice how Jimi fills in the gaps between the vocals every other measure with these figures throughout.

As is common with many Hendrix tunes, the mix throughout this song is absolutely essential in its effectiveness, and the verse demonstrates perfectly, as various guitar parts are pushed up in the mix for dramatic effect. This is most evident in measure 8 (Gtr. 2) and especially measure 10 (Gtr. 1).

Performance Tip: Jimi had fairly large hands, which facilitated the "Hendrix" style of riffing through chord shapes with hammer-ons and pull-offs. For those of us not blessed with this advantage, we're forced to compensate. While Jimi was able to play most of these figures with his thumb over the top of the neck, it may be necessary to adjust your thumb position between the two extremes (over the neck and behind the neck), depending on the particular passage.

2 Full Band

3 Slow Demo
Gtr. 2 meas. 1–4

Fig. 2

Figure 3—Guitar Solo 1

After the first verse, Jimi takes a quick eight-measure solo filled to the brim with expressive techniques. Again, he draws mostly from the C♯ minor pentatonic scale, occasionally spicing it up with a few extra notes. Notice how the rhythm guitar (Gtr. 1) has moved back into a more active strumming role to support the energy of the solo. He opens with a classic rock staple: the unison bend. Grab the B note with your third finger and bend up a whole step to match the C♯ note held by your first finger on string 1. Notice that on beat 3 the G string is incidentally sounded briefly during the release of the bend. (We will see instances throughout this book in which Hendrix makes intentional use of this technique to great effect.)

In measure 3 he moves up into the extended box position and revisits a motive found in the intro solo: the tonic bent up a whole step to the 9th (D♯). He pushes the envelope a bit further here, though, by stretching an additional half step to create a minor 3rd bend from C♯ to E. Notice how almost all of these bends are treated to Hendrix's lyrical trademark vibrato. He wraps up the solo in measure 7 with a sixteenth-note lick from the C♯ minor pentatonic box in ninth position, making use of a few half-step bends along the way for a bluesy touch. Although none of these lines are particularly difficult, it's Hendrix's touch and tone that make them shine, effectively illustrating that the man's playing was about much more than just flashiness. If you took away all of his pyrotechnics and showiness, you'd still be left with a *really* good guitar player.

4 Full Band

5 Slow Demo
Gtr. 2 meas. 7–8

Figure 4—Guitar Solo 2 and Interlude

Hendrix continues to work from the ninth-position C♯ minor pentatonic box in the second solo, again making extensive use of bends (including a few unison bends) throughout. He divides the solo evenly, moving up into the extended position at measure 5 and remaining there. He pulls out a lick from the B.B. King book in measure 6, following a pre-bent F♯ note with an E note bent up a whole step with the first finger. It may take a bit of practice to accomplish this if you're not used to bending with the first finger, so take your time with it.

Hendrix continues with a spacey interlude featuring a slide part played on an electric 12-string (Gtr. 3). Gtr. 1 switches gears again for this section, using mostly half-note strums to provide a more ethereal mood. Treated to a liberal amount of delay and constant panning from side to side, Gtr. 3 highlights melodic tones from the C♯ minor pentatonic scale with slow, glassy, deliberate articulation. The result is nothing short of brilliant, luring the listener into sonic dreamland before the song is re-energized with the following solo.

Fig. 4

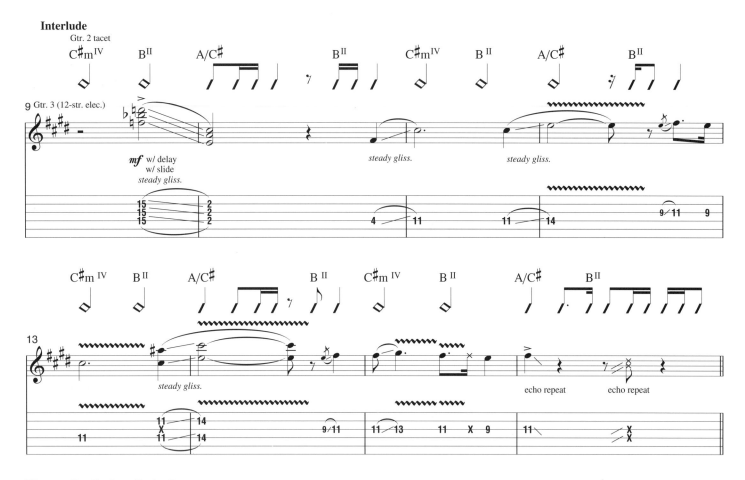

Figure 5—Guitar Solo 3

Hendrix's musical genius simply shines in the third solo. He begins by kicking on the wah wah and climbing up the C♯ minor pentatonic scale in sixteenth-note octaves. He follows this in measure 3 with a sixteenth-note line out of home base: the C♯ minor pentatonic scale in ninth position. He remains in this position for the sixteenth-note lick in measures 5–6, but he includes the hip 9th (D♯) note for a hexatonic scale sound (C♯–D♯–E–F♯–G♯–B). He finishes off this eight-measure section with two unison bends: C♯ over C♯m in measure 7, and D♯ over A in measure 8, resulting in a colorful Lydian (♯4) tonality. Throughout these first eight measures, the articulation of the wah wah pedal results in a beautiful, lazy, behind-the-beat feeling that grabs the attention of the listener and doesn't let go. It's a real lesson in how the rhythmic phrasing of a line can add a whole new dimension to a phrase.

Hendrix turns off the wah for the second section of the solo, which turns out to be the most unique-sounding guitar work in the song. Working from the top two strings of an E barre chord shape, Hendrix creates a descending double-stop motive that alternates the 9th and tonic over the 5th for each of the C♯m and B chords. He moves this same double-stop shape down again for the A chord, but abandons the 9th/tonic approach for something even more interesting and ear-grabbing. Here he moves to strings 2 and 3 and slides up into an E/G double stop, implying a bluesy A7 tonality, an unheard sound as of yet. He moves this 5th/♭7th double stop up a step to F♯/A for the B chord in beat 3, punctuating beat 4 with an A/C♯ dyad—the ♭7th and ♭9th of B! Measure 11 is essentially a repeat of measure 9 (with slight variation), but he changes things up again for measure 12. As if not to wear out his newfound harmonic interpretations so quickly, Hendrix fills out the remainder of the measure with a barrage of muted sixteenth-note strums for a purely rhythmic effect. Measures 13–14 are essentially a repeat of 9–10, and Jimi rounds out the section with a series of ascending unison bends that climb through the C♯ minor pentatonic scale. This results in an eight-measure phrase that makes effective use of the "question-answer" approach, repeating earlier parts of the phrase with alternate endings each time. Make sure and notice the difference that the rock-solid rhythmic delivery plays in this section when contrasted with the first eight measures of the solo. Brilliant, brilliant, brilliant!

Fig. 5

Guitar Solo

ANGEL
(*First Rays of the New Rising Sun*, 1997)
Words and Music by Jimi Hendrix

Appearing on the posthumous *First Rays of the New Rising Sun* album from 1997, "Angel" adds to the list of beautiful ballads penned by the guitarist. As there is no solo proper in this song, Hendrix's formidable rhythm chops are granted center stage.

Figure 6—Intro and Verse

"Angel" opens with a clean-toned electric (treated with a Leslie speaker effect) arpeggiating through some colorful chords that make use of both (low and high) open E strings as drones. Notice how the fretted portion of the lush Emaj9 shape is simply moved down a whole step in measure 2 to form the A6/E. This moving of a chord shape among droning open strings is a common guitar technique that can be found in countless guitar-driven songs, such as "Melissa" by the Allman Brothers.

In the second half of measure 3, Hendrix moves the fretted C#m7 voicing (C#–E–B) up a whole step to form the bright-sounding C#m11/E cluster, which, when including the open E string on top, contains the notes D#, E, and F# in the same register. He rounds out the intro with two measures of the A6/E chord, mixing eighth- and sixteenth-note arpeggio patterns.

Performance Tip: The long, wavy line at the beginning of measures 1–4 indicates that you should brush through the strings from low to high in one continuous stroke, but not as quickly as a standard strum. The effect should be one in which strings 6–2 almost sound like grace notes leading to string 1 on the downbeat.

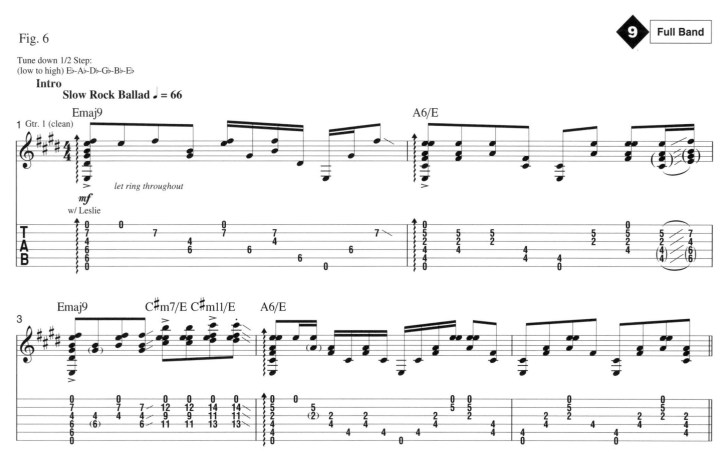

Fig. 6

9 Full Band

Figure 7—Verse

In a stroke of compositional brilliance, Jimi modulates up a whole step to the key of F♯ for the verse, effectively adding a slight lift in energy to the new section. The verse is a thirteen-measure section comprised of three four-measure phrases and a one-measure extension on the end. The first phrase (measures 1–4) is built upon an F♯–C♯6, G♯m7, B–E, F♯–C♯–B progression, and Hendrix varies his rhythmic approach throughout to keep things interesting.

In measure 1, he arpeggiates through the chords in a manner similar to the intro, but he riffs through the G♯m7 chord in measure 2 in typical Hendrix fashion, finishing off in beat 4 with a chromatically-descending line that leads to the root of the B chord in the next measure. After strumming through the B, he treats the E and F♯ chords to sliding 6ths on strings 3 and 1, and finishes off the phrase by sliding the C♯ barre chord down a whole step to B.

Measures 5–8 repeat the same progression with one exception: an E chord replaces the C♯ and B at the end of the phrase. Hendrix treats this repeated phrase similarly to the first, varying his fill for the G♯m7 chord and extending the 6ths approach through the E chord at the end of the phrase.

The final five measures feature a colorful progression of B5–D5, F♯, G♯m–A♯m, B, Bsus4. While we have had one *non-diatonic* chord (a chord outside the key) thus far—E— we also see another in this phrase: D major. Both of these two chords are known as *borrowed* chords, because they are said to be "borrowed" from the parallel key of F♯ minor. This kind of harmonic technique is called *modal mixture*, and it shows up all over the place in Hendrix's music. After essentially strumming through B5, D5, and F♯ in measures 9–10 Jimi puts his thumb to use on the sixth string and transposes a similar riff for the G♯m up a whole step to cover the A♯m. The final two measures, B–Bsus4, serve as an extended build-up to the approaching chorus.

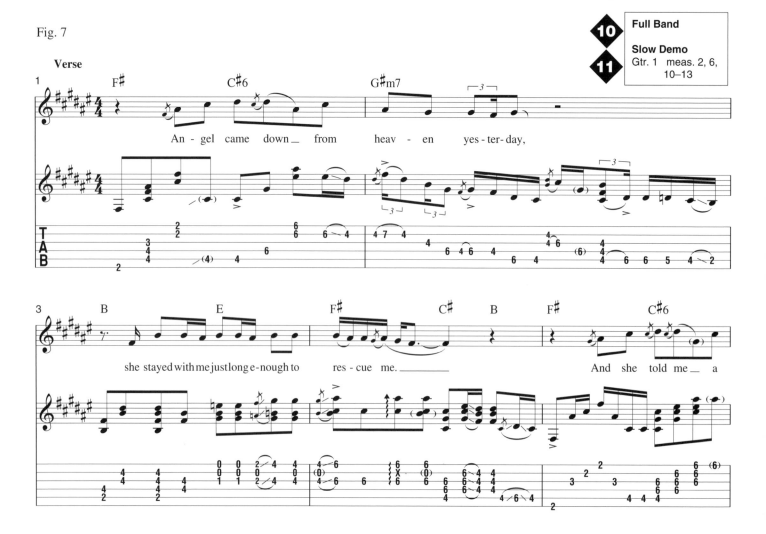

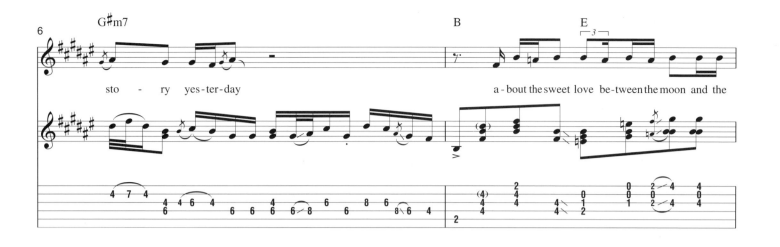

sto - ry yes-ter-day

a - bout the sweet love be-tween the moon and the

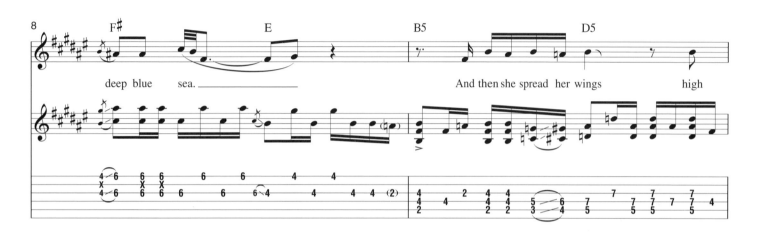

deep blue sea._____

And then she spread her wings

high

o - ver me._____

She said, she's go-ing to

come back to -

*T = Thumb on 6th string

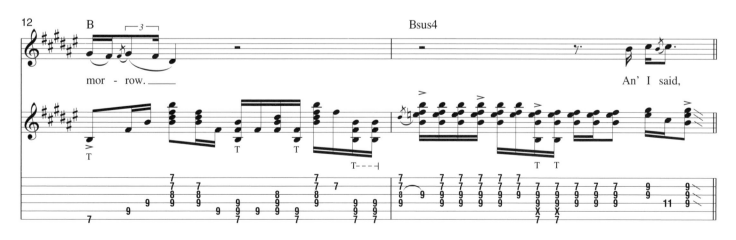

mor - row._____

An' I said,

Figure 8—Chorus and Interlude

While the extended Bsus4 chord at the end of the verse may have sounded a little strange at first, its purpose is revealed fully with the arrival of the chorus. Here, we've modulated again, back to the key of E, which was home in the intro. The B chord could be seen as a V chord in the key of E. When a chord can be analyzed as diatonic in two different keys (B is IV in F♯ and V in E), it is known as a *pivot chord*. The use of a pivot chord usually results in much smoother key changes.

The chorus features another colorful chord progression that makes use of modal mixture. Measures 1 and 2 are harmless enough, as Jimi employs the same droning open-string trick found in the intro for the E and F♯m11 chords. Measure 3, however, changes chords on each beat for a C–A–D–D♯ progression. The C to A move is especially ear-catching, as the C chord, borrowed from E minor, is immediately followed by the diatonic IV (A) chord, which contains the note C♯. The D chord, again borrowed from E minor, makes its way back to the tonic E chord in measure 4 by way of a chromatic D♯ chord. Hendrix treats the E chord to some chord-melody riffing that includes a bluesy G♮ passing tone in beat 3.

This four-measure phrase is essentially repeated with two exceptions. In measure 6 Hendrix fills in the gap between vocal phrases in beats 3–4 with a sixteenth-note melody (F♯–G♯–F♯–E), stated with typical grace and ease. After one more statement (sans vocals) of the C–A–D–D♯ progression, he embarks on a brief interlude that returns to the droning open-string theme of the intro. Here, however, he moves the fretted E major shape on strings 5–3 diatonically up to the F♯m shape, creating F♯m11, and follows with a G major shape, which creates an Em7 borrowed chord. This is followed by a return to the F♯m11, which is extended to two measures, with a ritard in tempo, that leads to the next verse (not shown).

Fig. 8

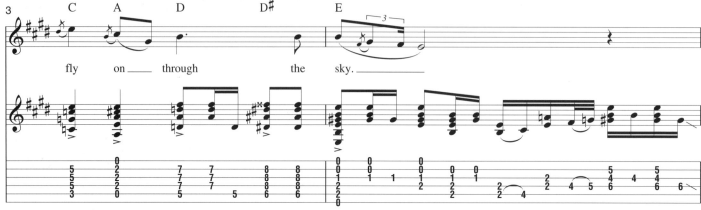

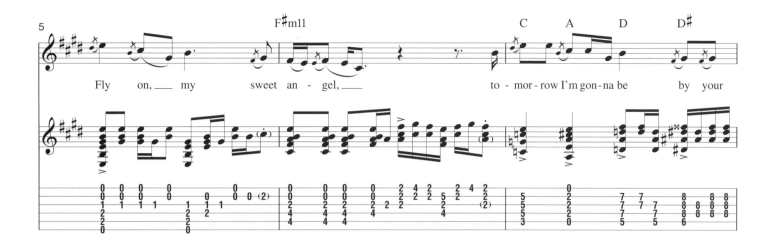

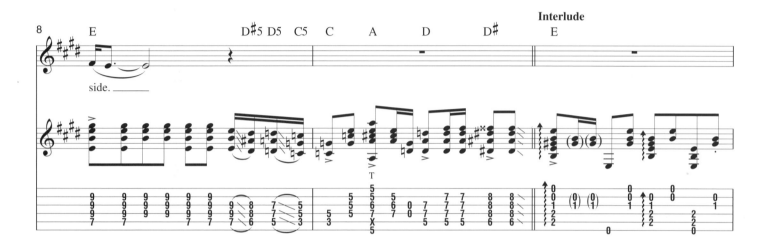

Figure 9—Chorus 2 and Outro

For the second chorus, Hendrix varies his approach in several spots worthy of mention. In measure 4 he caps off the first phrase with an elegant triple-stop riff on beats 3–4 in which he descends the scale on string 5 from A to F♯ against a B and E held on strings 4 and 3, respectively. He decorates the following E chord in measure 5 with a first-inversion (3rd on bottom) A chord shape in ninth position. He descends from the F♯ minor harmony in measure 4 to the C chord in measure 7 by way of a sixteenth-note run on beat 4 (F♯–E–D♯–D♮); this riff is then altered to (E–D♯–D♮–C♯) for the E chord in measure 8. It appears again in measure 10 with the last C♯ note replaced with an open A string.

At measure 12 we get a surprise move to F♯ for the outro. After strumming through F♯ and A chords in measures 12 and 13, respectively, Hendrix moves to slowly ascending octaves over a progression of C♯, F♯, A, A, C♯, C♯ (implied by the bass). At measure 20, things finally get grounded again on a D major harmony, and Hendrix begins a two-measure syncopated phrase built from descending octaves through the D major scale and repeats this through the fadeout.

Fig. 9

18

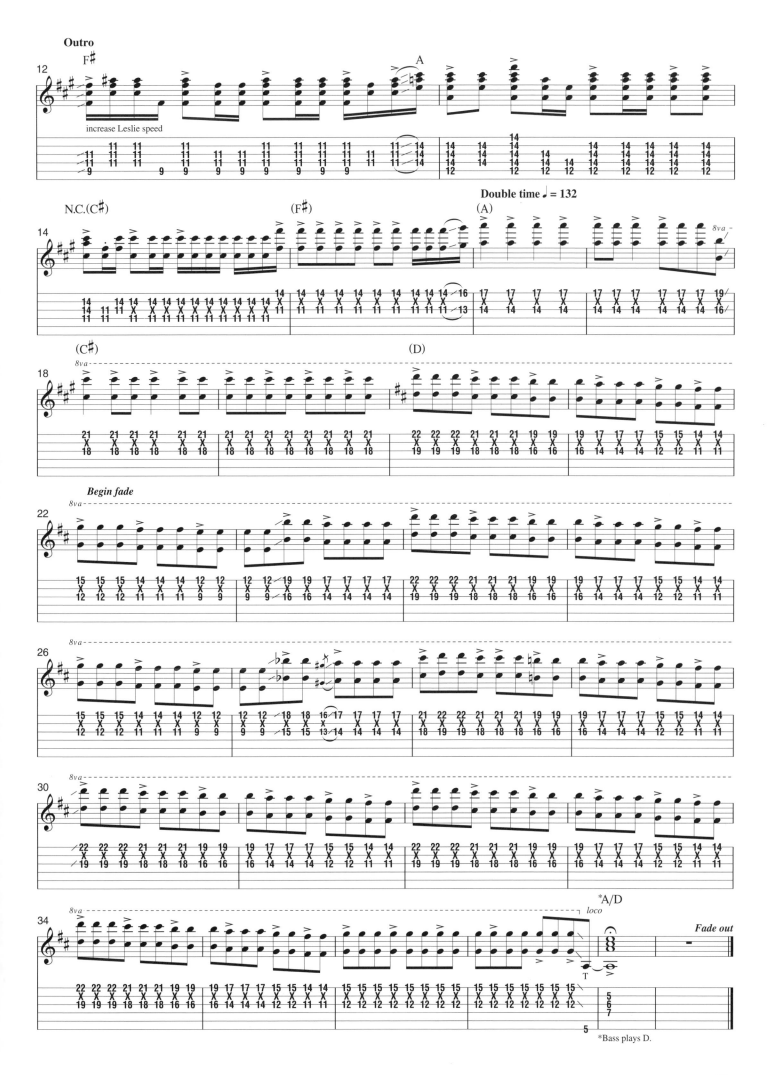

THE BURNING OF THE MIDNIGHT LAMP

(*Electric Ladyland*, 1968)

Words and Music by Jimi Hendrix

Recorded at Mayfair Studios, New York, in July of 1967, "The Burning of the Midnight Lamp" featured a unique instrumentation that was further augmented by the Sweet Inspirations on back-up vocals (who had appeared earlier on "Hey Joe"). Modulatory chord progressions, layered guitar parts, and poetic lyrics all combine in "Midnight Lamp" to form another classic Hendrix tune.

Figure 10—Intro

The tune begins with an instrumental theme elegantly stated by Jimi's wahed guitar (Gtr. 1) and... what else?... harpsichord, of course! The sound is unique to say the least, but of course that's pretty much par for the course when you're talking about Hendrix.

The theme is based in C major and consists of a repeating eighth-note melody in which the first note is altered each measure to imply a C–F–B♭–C (I–IV–♭VII–I) progression. The four-measure phrase wraps up with a sixteenth-note lick that begins on and surrounds the note E. Notice the grace notes used throughout the theme that coincide with the Baroque tinge lent by the harpsichord's presence.

The bass and drums enter at measure 5, and the theme is repeated verbatim to form an eight-measure intro. Jimi lets us know things are getting under way in measure 8 with an overdubbed part (Gtr. 2) that combines a tremolo-bar dive with a fluttered wah-wah effect for a typical otherworldly Hendrix flavor.

Fig. 10

16 Full Band

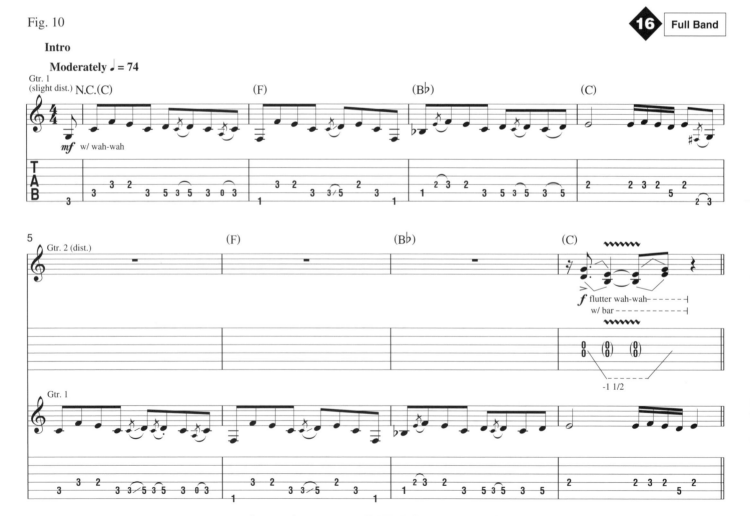

Figure 11—Verse and Chorus

The verse begins with a key change to F major, but it doesn't stay there long. If we consider only the prominent chords throughout the verse, F–Dm–B–E–C–G–D–F, we've covered at least the keys of F (measures 1–2), E (measures 3–4), and G (measures 5–8). (Technically, the F chord in measure 8 doesn't belong to the key of G, but it can be analyzed as a ♭VII chord since its purpose seems to be the approach to the G chord by way of a chromatic F♯.)

Gtr. 3 chirps out staccato chords on beats 2 and 4, while Gtr. 1 strums through most of the chords, occasionally adding a few hammer-on embellishments as in measures 3, 5, and 6. Measure 5 is particularly noteworthy, as it highlights a favorite embellishment of Hendrix. This involves moving from a root-position, fretted A major-type barre chord based on string 5 (C major in this case), in which your third finger is barring, to its first inversion form in which your first finger is performing the barre while your other fingers hammer on and pull off embellishments. Two common embellishments, the 5th to 6th and 2nd to 3rd, appear in this measure, but Hendrix also makes use of many more. These may include the root on string 3 hammered to the 9th, the ♭3rd on string 5 with the middle finger hammered to the 3rd with the ring finger, and the 3rd on string 2 hammered to either the 4th or 5th with the second or fourth fingers, respectively.

For the chorus, which consists of alternating G and C/G chords, Gtr. 3 moves to 6ths picked hybrid style (with pick and fingers). These slowly climb up the fretboard to form various inversions and combine with the stratospheric background vocals in a musical climax.

Fig. 11

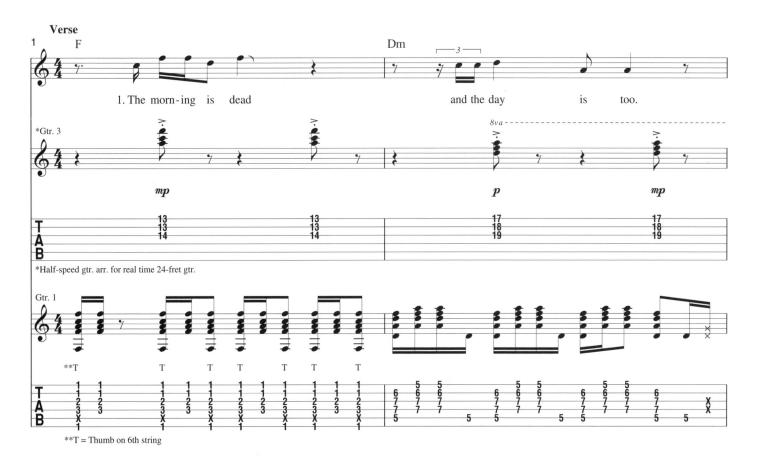

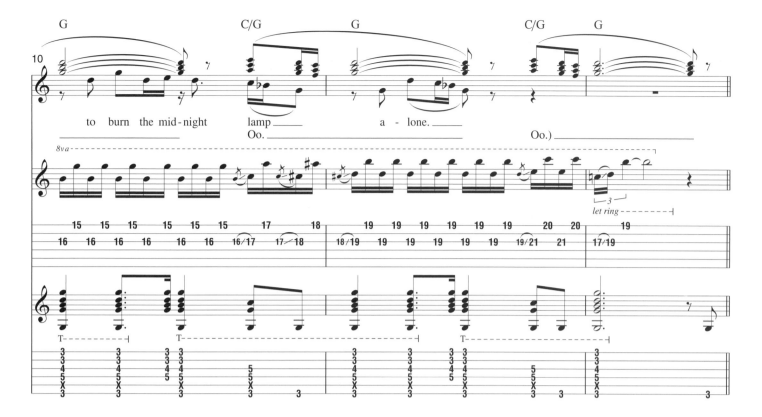

to burn the mid-night lamp _____ a - lone. _____
Oo. Oo.)

Figure 12—Guitar Solo

The solo begins over a new two-measure chord progression of B♭5–C5, G5, and Hendrix kicks it off in the pickup measure with a wah-wah fluttered lick from the G minor pentatonic scale (G–B♭–C–D–F) in fifteenth position. He works almost exclusively from this position and the one an octave lower at fret 3 throughout the solo, making extensive use of the fluttering wah effect several times. The only exception to the G minor pentatonic scale in the entire solo takes place during measure 7, where he briefly moves up to fifth position, hammers to and pulls off from the A note, and quickly slides back down to third position. He caps off the solo the same way he capped off the intro, with a wah-fluttered tremolo dive.

18 Full Band

19 Slow Demo
Gtr. 2 meas. 1–8

Fig. 12

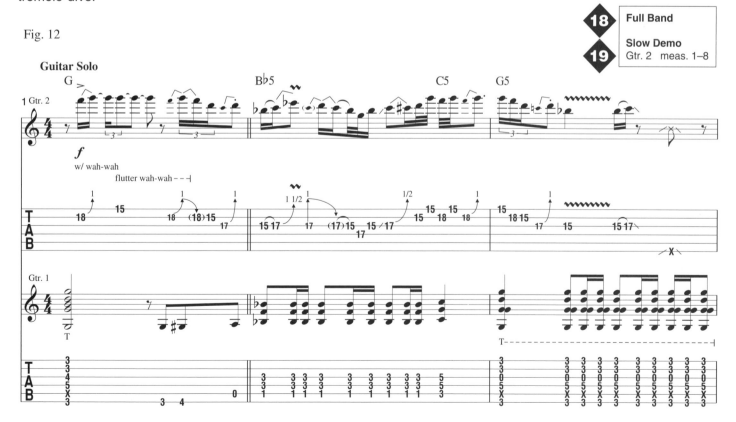

CROSSTOWN TRAFFIC
(*Electric Ladyland*, 1968)
Words and Music by Jimi Hendrix

Recorded in December of 1967, "Crosstown Traffic" appeared on 1968's *Electric Ladyland* and reached #52 on the U.S. charts. Evidently, Jimi was having trouble getting the lead guitar melody to sound like he envisioned. After doubling it with vocals, it still wasn't quite there. So, he improvised with a comb and cellophane to create a makeshift kazoo, which fit the bill nicely.

Figure 13—Intro

"Crosstown Traffic" begins with a two-measure syncopated figure that's accented by the entire band. Gtr. 1 wrenches out a string bending triple-stop figure from the C# minor pentatonic box in ninth position while Gtr. 3 pounds out a Bsus4 chord. The repetition of the sixteenth/eighth rhythm creates a sense of rhythmic ambiguity that lasts the entire two measures. Only on beat 4 of measure 2 do things become grounded with two eighth notes, allowing us to finally lock into the groove of the song at the downbeat of measure 3. Adding to the rhythmic disorientation is the fact that the entire mix slowly sweeps across the stereo spectrum from far left to far right throughout the riff.

At this point, we break into a three-guitar texture of the two-measure chord progression of C#m7–F#7#9 that serves as the basis of the interludes and choruses. Gtr. 1 (with fuzz and doubled by vocals and kazoo!) plays a catchy, blues melody based on the C# minor pentatonic scale (C#–E–F#–G#–B) at the ninth fret, while Gtr. 2 stomps out a bass melody that adds the chromatic tones B# and E# to the C# minor pentatonic scale. Gtr. 3 provides the harmonic support, alternating C#m7 and tart F#7#9 chords with similar voicing shapes. The Gtr. 4 part, which is essentially just pecking out bass notes on beats 1 and 3, is an arrangement for the ultra-compressed piano part. After this two-measure phrase is heard three times, the intro comes to a close with a two-measure syncopated Bsus4 phrase similar to the way the song began. Gtr. 2 heightens the anticipation during this phrase by sliding up the notes of the C# minor pentatonic scale on the third string against the droning open first and second strings.

Fig. 13

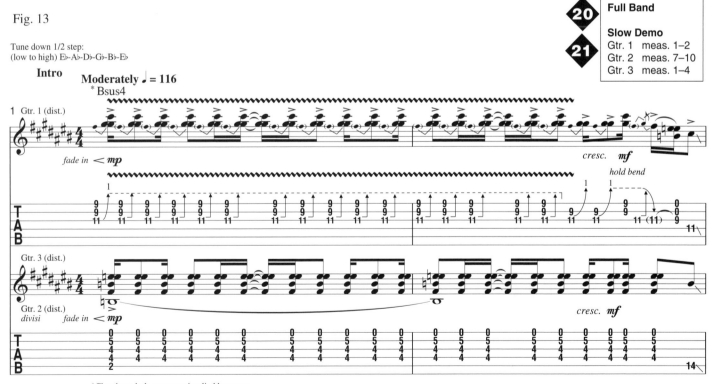

20 Full Band

21 Slow Demo
Gtr. 1 meas. 1–2
Gtr. 2 meas. 7–10
Gtr. 3 meas. 1–4

*Chord symbols represent implied harmony.

*Piano arranged for gtr.　　　　**Gtr. 4 tabbed to right.

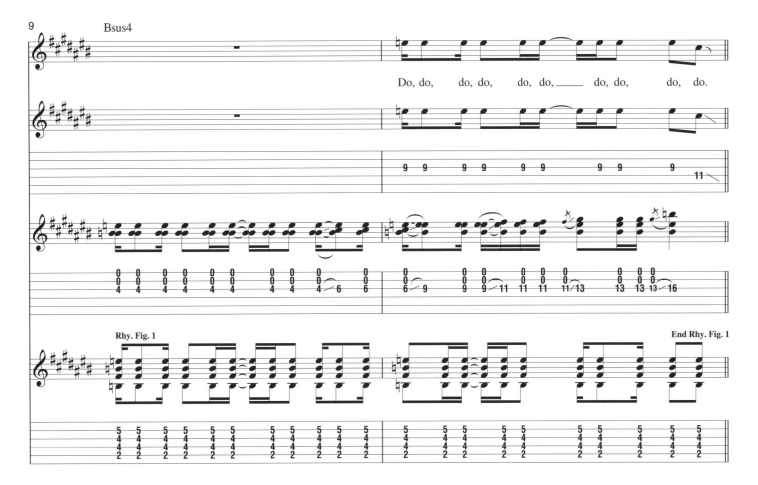

Figure 14—Verse

The verse features a dramatic change in texture, with only Gtr. 2 banging out chords on the first two eighth notes of each measure, allowing the drums and vocals to take center stage. The tonic chord also changes here from C#m7 to C#7, creating a nastier edge to the proceedings to which the drums respond with a funkier beat. After twice through the new C#7–F#7 progression, a new, slightly jazz-influenced progression takes over the final measures of the verse: Bm7–E7–Am7–G#7. Notice that the first three chords progress by the interval of a 5th: Bm7 is a 5th down from the previous F#7, E7 is a 5th from Bm7, and Am7 is a 5th from E7. These circle-of-5ths progressions are extremely popular in jazz, a style in which Jimi certainly had become interested. The 5th movement is abandoned after the Am7, as we slide down a half step to G#7 in order to set up the return to C#m7 at the beginning of the approaching chorus. The familiar sixteenth/eighth-note syncopated figure is heard here again, and the verse is stretched out an extra measure to heighten the tension. For measure 9, the guitar texture thickens fully again to include the kazoo/vocal-doubled Gtr. 1 and Gtr. 3.

◆22	**Full Band**
◆23	**Slow Demo**
	Gtr. 1 meas. 9
	Gtr. 2 meas. 8–9

Fig. 14

*T = Thumb on 6th string

Figure 15—Chorus 2 and Interlude

The chorus sections are orchestrated similarly to the intro, with Gtr. 1 providing C♯ minor pentatonic melodies to fill in the gaps between vocal phrases, Gtr. 2 providing a low-register bassline riff, and Gtr. 3 banging out the chords. However, notice that Gtr. 1's melodies have shifted to the even-numbered measures here, as the vocal phrases appear primarily in the odd-numbered measures. This is a subtle, yet effective way to recycle previously-used material while making it sound fresh. Also note that Hendrix alters the second melody to keep things interesting, finishing off with a vibratoed bend in measure 5. The two-measure Bsus4 phrase is again used to round out the section, but Jimi treats this one slightly differently in terms of guitar work. Gtr. 2 employs a bass-chord approach for measure 7 with a bit of chromatic side-slipping at the end. Note, however, that this is a C♯7 chord he's playing, which results in quite a dense wall of sound against the Bsus4 chord played by Gtr. 3 (Rhy. Fig. 1). He adds to the sonic "traffic jam" in measure 8 by moving various dyads on strings 4 and 3 (4ths, tritones, and 5ths) down the fretboard in a syncopated rhythm.

The tension is released at the beginning of the next measure with the interlude, a four-measure phrase that briefly tonicizes the 5th, G♯. The texture here is also similar to the intro and choruses. Gtr. 2 riffs with alternating bass-chord style, centered around G♯7, while Gtr. 1 now works from the G♯ minor pentatonic scale (G♯–B–C♯–D♯–F♯) to create the lead melodies.

Fig. 15

*Gtr. 4 tabbed to right.

Figure 16—Outro Chorus

For the outro chorus, Hendrix combines several previously heard elements in different ways, resulting in another fresh treatment that keeps the listener's attention. Things begin harmlessly enough, but notice now that Gtr. 1 has moved back to phrasing on the odd-numbered measures, just as was heard in the intro. We're then thrown a curve ball in measure 3, as the chorus is seemingly cut short with the arrival of the two-measure, syncopated Bsus4 figure. Gtr. 1 riffs through this phrase by moving down through various notes of a C#m7 chord (B, E, C#, and B). The chorus returns in measure 5, however, only to be interrupted again at measure 7 with the Bsus4 figure again. This time it's only one measure long, and Gtr. 1 pulls off a Jeff Beck-like figure that mixes half- and whole-step bends to and from the B note. After the chorus returns in measures 8 and 9, Gtr. 1 snakes its way through another Bsus4 break (two measures long this time) by alternating an unbent F# note with one bent a whole step to G# in the alternating sixteenth/eighth-note syncopation for a hiccupping rhythmic effect. As if Hendrix suspects that we're finally on to his phrase-rotating trick, the song fades out.

This section serves as a prime example of clever arranging. While so many pop songs seem to reach a point of utter predictability with a repeating chorus at the end, "Traffic" demonstrates that songs need not always reach a point of automatic pilot when there are no more new musical sections to be heard.

Fig. 16

Outro Chorus

*Gtr. 4 tabbed to right.

DOLLY DAGGER
(*First Rays of the New Rising Sun*, 1997)
Words and Music by Jimi Hendrix

"Dolly Dagger," which appeared on the posthumous *First Rays of the New Rising Sun*, was actually conceived with the sounds of a famous clock tower in mind. One day in August of 1969, bassist Billy Cox was imitating the chimes of Big Ben on his bass. Hendrix rushed outside, grabbed his guitar, and the two worked out the intro to what would become "Dolly Dagger." For the song, Hendrix's guitar was recorded in stereo, combining the direct signal from his guitar with that of his amplifier.

Figure 17—Intro and Chorus 1

After five beats of percussion, the song kicks off with the Big Ben-inspired riff played in octaves by Gtrs. 1 & 2. This tone is thickened even more by Cox's distorted bass, resulting in a massive, fuzzy texture. The riff's origins are disguised quite nicely by the upbeat tempo, but if you play the first four notes (F#–D–E–A) slowly, the clock chime is obvious. This phrase (in the slightly unusual 6/4 meter) is imitated by a similar phrase that begins a 4th lower. This follows exactly the same contour as the first phrase save for the last note. A 4/4 phrase from the B Blues scale (B–D–E–F–F#–A) rounds out the intro.

The chorus centers mostly around the tonic chord (B), with a quick shift to E (implied by the bass) in measures 2 and 5. Hendrix plants his thumb on the low sixth-string B note and creates a beautifully complementary guitar part in measures 1–2, combining chords, bass octaves, and bluesy double-stop bends from the B Dorian mode (B–C#–D–E–F#–G#–A). In measure 3, Hendrix and Cox launch into a two-measure syncopated phrase that's built upon three-note ascending chromatic groupings played in straight eighth notes: D–D#–E, A–A#–B, E–F#–F#, and A–A#–B. Hendrix made use of similar figures earlier in "Hey Joe" and "Manic Depression." This riff represents a fresh adaptation, however, with the three-over-four syncopation at work. The chorus finishes off with another statement of the intro figure (with the first F# note "bluesified" to F#), thickened further with the overdubbed Gtr. 2's percussive clicks.

Fig. 17

Figure 18—Verse

Hendrix's rhythm chops shine once again for the verse, as he demonstrates his mastery of various chord voicings spanning the neck. Using an infectious, imitative, sixteenth-note strumming rhythm, he doesn't stay in one place for long, grabbing B, B7, and B9 voicings along the way. What's more, Hendrix varies the placement of these different voicings throughout, creating a part that keeps the listener guessing every two beats. At the end of measures 4, 8, 10, 12, 14, and 16, Jimi joins bassist Billy Cox for a two-beat B minor pentatonic riff that helps inject new energy throughout the one-chord verse.

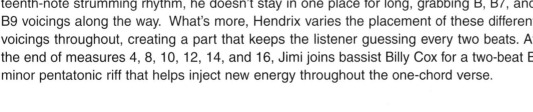

Fig. 18

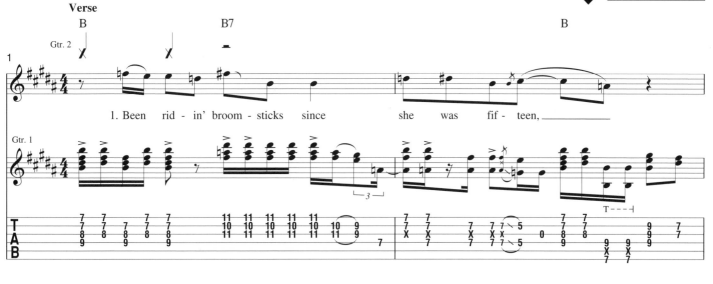

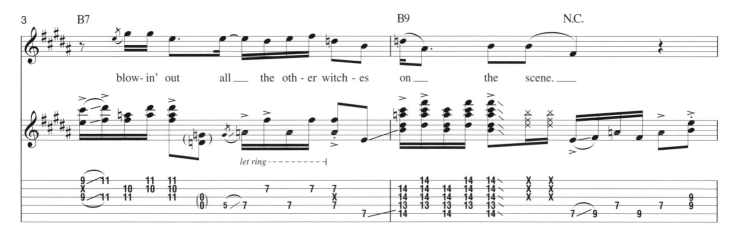

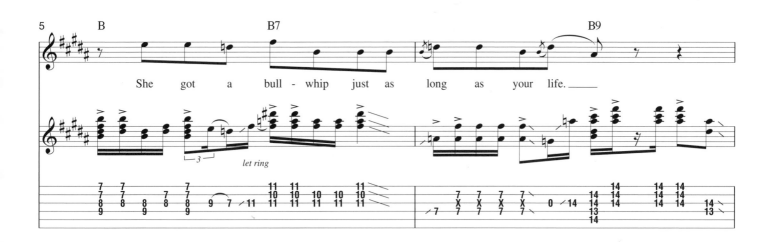

Figure 19—Guitar Solo

After the second chorus (not shown), Jimi takes a sixteen-measure solo over the one-chord verse form. For measures 1–8, Hendrix works almost exclusively from the B minor pentatonic box shape in seventh position, mixing all degrees of bends throughout. The only exception includes his deliberate inclusion of the F♮ note in measure 4 from the B Blues scale. Highlights include the two-and-a-half-step bend from E to A in measure 5 and the alternating one-and-a-half-step and two-step bends from the D note in measures 6–8, all of which serve tribute to one of Jimi's idols, blues legend Albert King.

In measures 9 and 10 Hendrix spices up his sixteenth-note lines with a bluesy hammer-on from the minor 3rd (D) to the major 3rd (D♯), and in measure 11 follows a Blues scale descent with a quick pentatonic climb up into the extended box position in tenth position, where he executes more King-inspired bends.

In the second half of measure 12 he slides up farther to twelfth position and approaches the tonic B note by way of the 6th (G♯). He follows this with a few bends from F♯ up to G♯ and A, nodding again to the King—this time B.B. King. (Hendrix was well aware of the three "kings" of the blues: Albert, B.B., and Freddy.)

32 Full Band

33 Slow Demo
Gtr. 2 meas. 9–12

Fig. 19

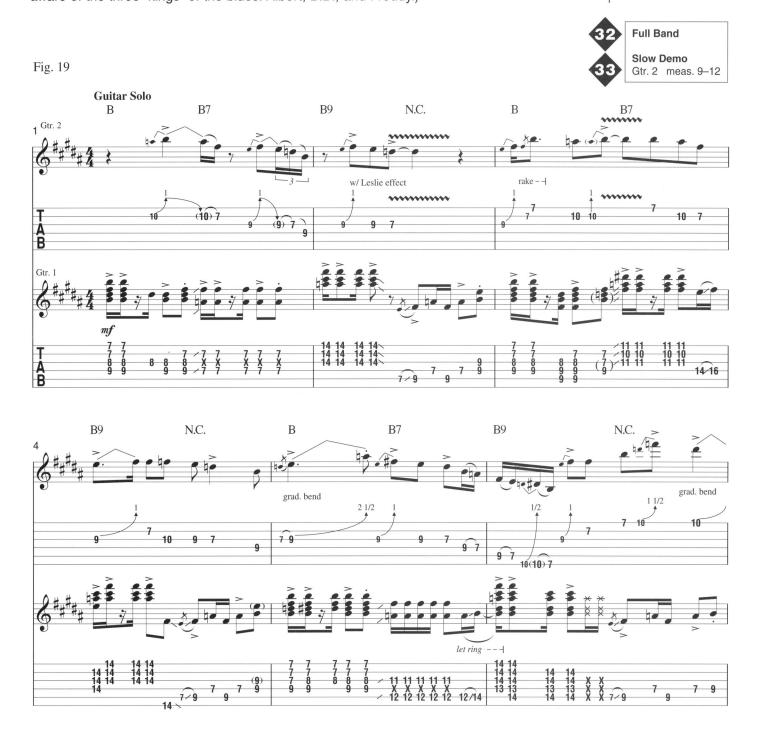

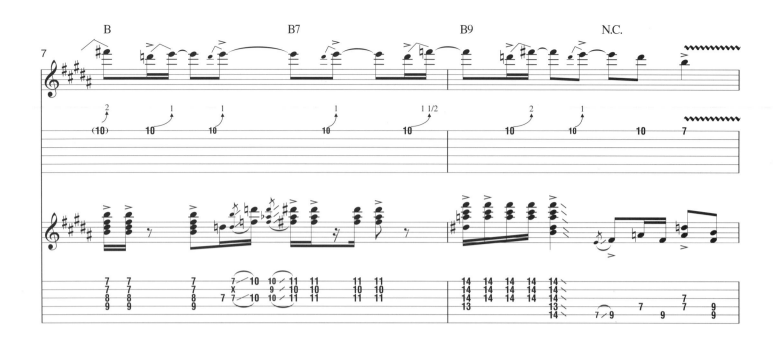

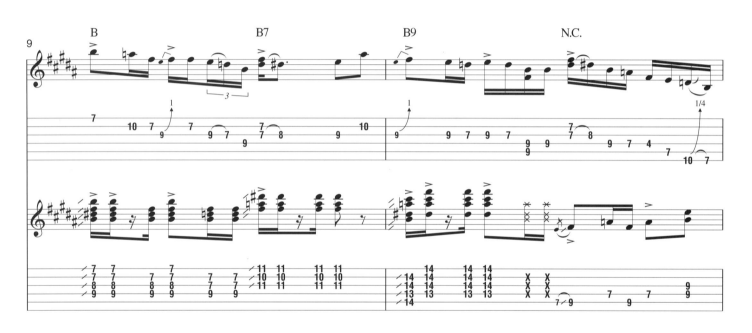

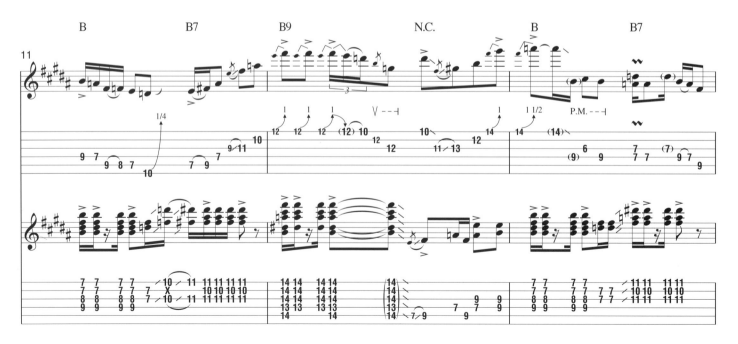

Figure 20—Chorus 3

In another display of brilliant arrangement and orchestration, Hendrix dramatically thins out the texture for the third chorus. Gtr. 1 replaces the chords and octaves in the previous choruses with effective, droning, double-stop bends throughout measures 1 and 5. Gtr. 2 provides muted, percussive clicks and tough, bluesy fills out of the B minor pentatonic scale.

Figure 21—Interlude and Outro

For the interlude, Hendrix again demonstrates his ability to recycle previously-used material to great effect. The 6/4 theme from the intro is adapted to a 4/4 meter here, with connective fills from E minor pentatonic (E–G–A–B–D) used to bridge the extra two-beat gap. The choice of E minor pentatonic is interesting here, as the song seems to have its foot in two different harmonic worlds at this point. Jimi solos over this section with Gtr. 2. He begins in measure 1 by briefly harmonizing with the theme in 5ths before launching into some blues licks from the B minor pentatonic scale. Jimi largely ignores the allusion to E minor pentatonic and, aside from the occasional C♯ note, sticks predominantly to B minor pentatonic or B Blues. At measure 9, the original intro theme in 6/4 is heard to close out the interlude.

For the outro that follows, Hendrix launches an eight-measure assault of double- and triple-stops from the B Dorian mode. At measure 20 he settles into nineteenth position and remains there through measure 43, combining blues licks with the occasional major 3rd bend from the C# at fret 21 on the first string. His lines here are reminiscent of Clapton's famous solo in "Crossroads." In measure 44 he drops down an octave to the seventh-position B minor pentatonic box and continues the bending frenzy, employing unison bends (measure 44) and oblique bends (measure 48). Toward the fade at measure 51, Hendrix launches into a sixteenth-note run on the bass strings that combines notes from the B Blues scale with the major 3rd (D#) at the end. Gtr. 1 supports the one-chord jam all along with muted percussive clicks, various B7 voicings, and counter-riffing from the B Blues scale and B Dorian mode.

Fig. 21

◆35 **Full Band**

◆36 **Slow Demo**
Gtr. 1 meas. 1–2, 30–33
Gtr. 2 meas. 12–19, 34–40

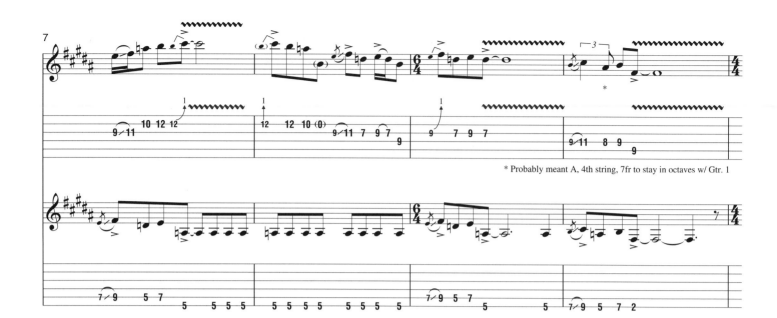

* Probably meant A, 4th string, 7fr to stay in octaves w/ Gtr. 1

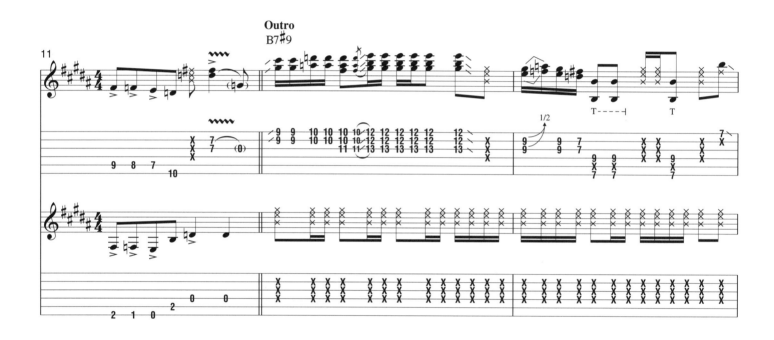

Outro
B7#9

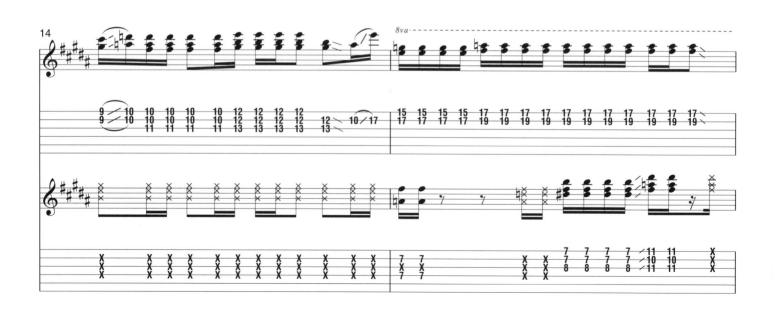

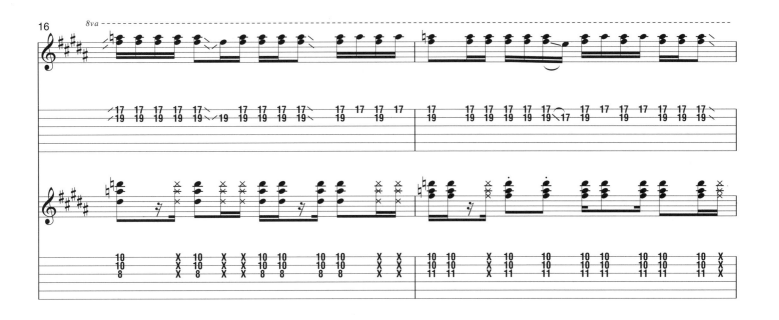

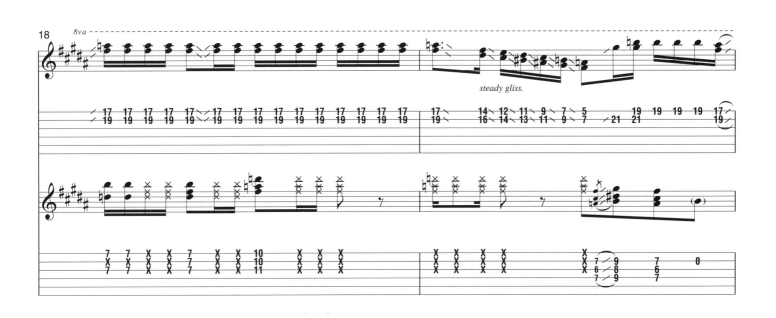

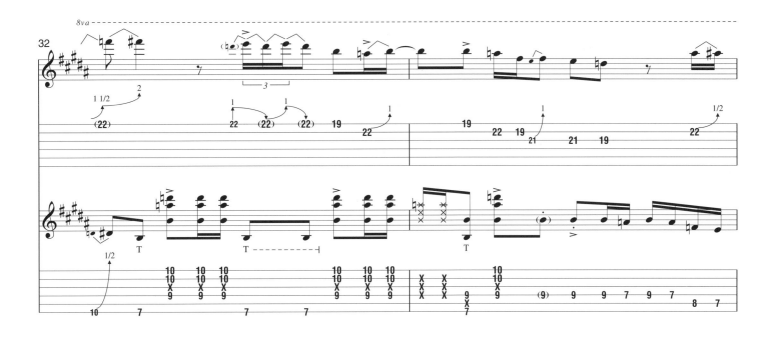

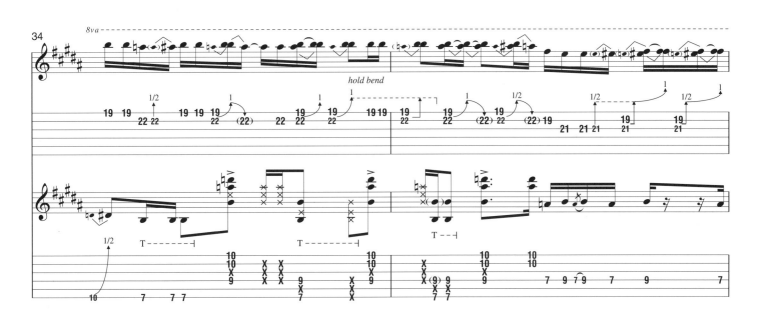

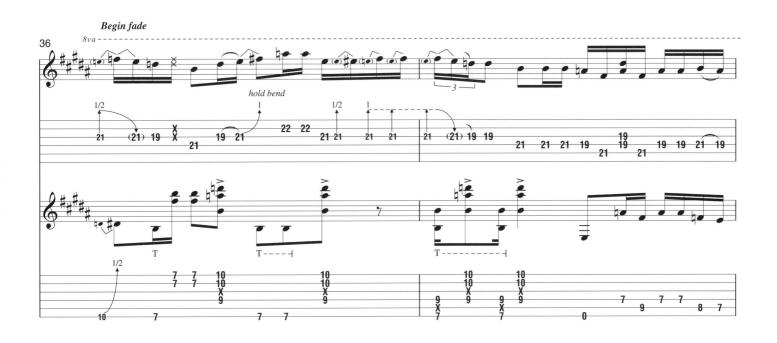

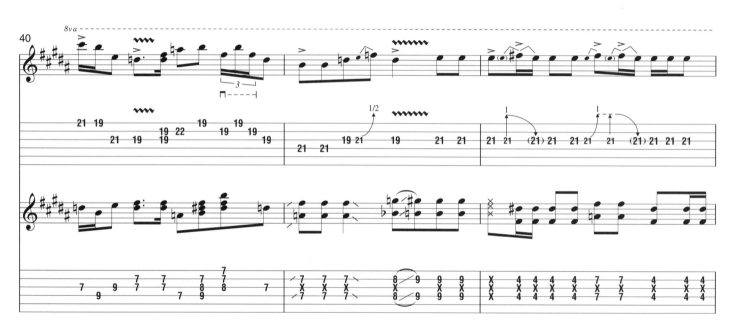

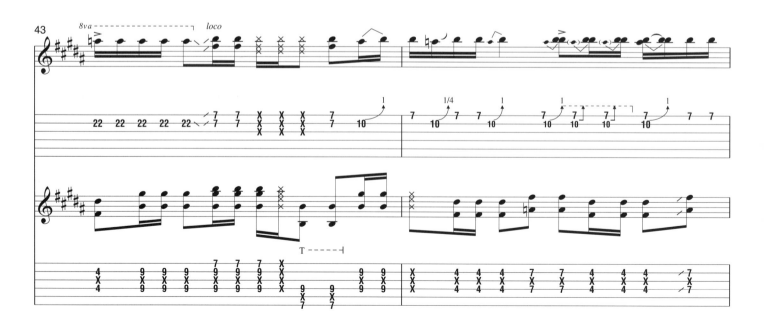

FREEDOM
(*First Rays of the New Rising Sun*, 1997)
Words and Music by Jimi Hendrix

Also released on *First Rays of the New Rising Sun*, "Freedom" was recorded in July of 1970. Slightly reminiscent of his earlier classic "Fire," the tune is a bluesy rocker just bursting with classic Hendrix guitar work.

Figure 22—Intro

Hendrix kicks off this tune with a ballsy guitar riff (Gtr. 1) with tone to spare. Many people through the years have commented endlessly on the "otherworldly" sounds Hendrix could coax out of the instrument, and while this is certainly true, he had no trouble getting stellar "worldly" sounds as well. There aren't any tricks to this tone; it's just flat-out perfect for the song. The riff, somewhat reminiscent of Albert King's "Born Under a Bad Sign," is built from the notes of the C♯ minor pentatonic scale (C♯–E–F♯–G♯–B) and combines power chords with a walking-style bass line. The fourth time through the riff, a reverb-drenched Gtr. 2 enters with a high bent F♯ note that's gradually released over a chromatically-descending bass line, both of which usher the band in for the downbeat of measure 5.

At measure 5, Gtr. 1 (left side) moves into a funkier riff consisting of double stops and single notes from the C♯m pentatonic scale, which basically suggests a C♯m7 tonality. Gtr. 3 (panned hard right) adds to the funkiness with clean-toned double stops, triads, and single notes centered around twelfth position and consisting mostly of the notes B and E, reinforcing the C♯m7 sound.

Gtr. 2 continues working from the extended C♯ minor pentatonic box in twelfth position through measure 7. In measure 8 he moves down to the standard box position to pull off a descending triplet lick that begins with a classic Hendrix move: the ♭7th (B) on string 2 bent a whole step followed by the ♭5th (G♮) *prebent* a half step and then released. This entire intro solo is filled with Albert King influence—even down to the stinging tone that Hendrix achieves.

Performance Tip: For beat 1 of measure 8 (Gtr. 2), bend the B note with your third finger and allow the G string to get caught underneath. Roll your third finger down to the G string and pick the note while the string is still bent a half step. Hendrix used this lick quite often and always fingered it this way.

Fig. 22

Tune down 1/2 step:
(low to high) E♭-A♭-D♭-G♭-B♭-E♭

37 | **Full Band**
38 | **Slow Demo** Gtr. 1 meas. 2 / Gtr. 2 meas. 8

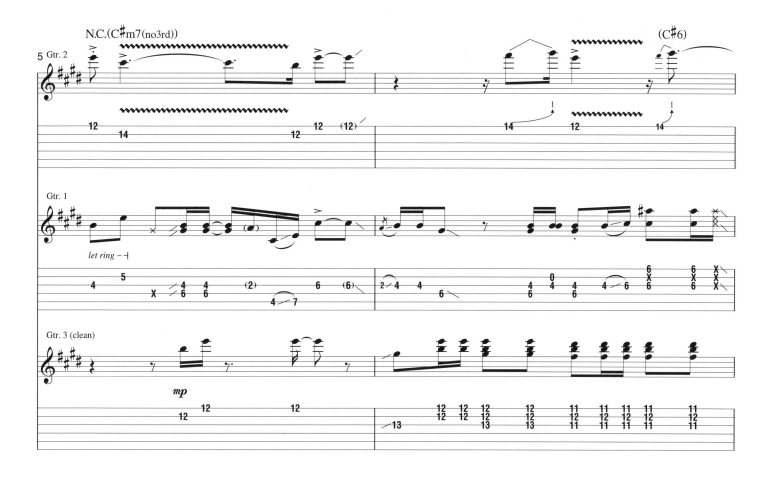

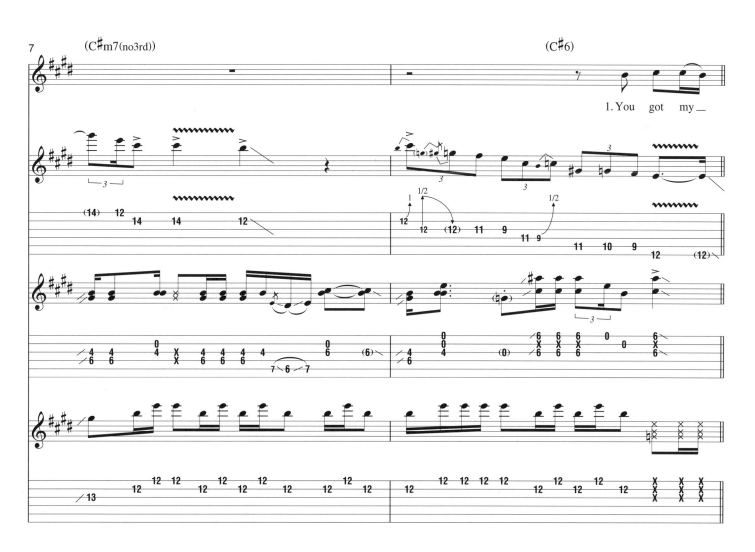

Figure 23—Verse

The verse maintains the three-guitar texture, but the parts thin out to leave room for the vocals. Gtr. 1 provides the backbone with a funky part that alternates between the Hendrix-approved C#7#9 voicing and C#9 with the occasional double-stop slide from B/E to C#/F#. Gtr. 3 adopts a purely rhythmic role using only percussive muted accents on the top strings, while Gtr. 2 fills throughout, working from the C# minor pentatonic scale.

Fig. 23

Figure 24—Chorus and Interlude

The chorus represents the first real harmonic variety from the C♯ tonality, but it doesn't stray too far. Gtr. 1 bashes out E chords on the first beat of each measure and fills the rest of them with single-note lines and double-stop riffs from the C♯ Dorian mode (C♯–D♯–E–F♯–G♯–A♯–B), allowing a piano to handle the main chordal duties. Gtr. 2 alternates a single bent and released B-note answer to the "Freedom" vocal refrain with E chords at the beginning of every other measure. Considering the combined sound created, the E chords sound almost more like C♯m7 chords in first inversion, thus maintaining the one-chord jam sound of the tune so far.

After the chorus, Gtr. 1 lays down the foundation for the four-measure interlude with a downright funky riff built from the C♯m pentatonic box in ninth position. Gtr. 2 adds some blazing lines atop it in measures 1–3 from the same position, moving up to the extended box in measure 4 to finish the section with some gut-wrenching bends, including a one-and-a-half-step bend on beat 4. Get it, Jimi!

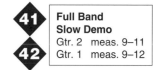

41 **Full Band Slow Demo** Gtr. 2 meas. 9–11
42 Gtr. 1 meas. 9–12

Fig. 24

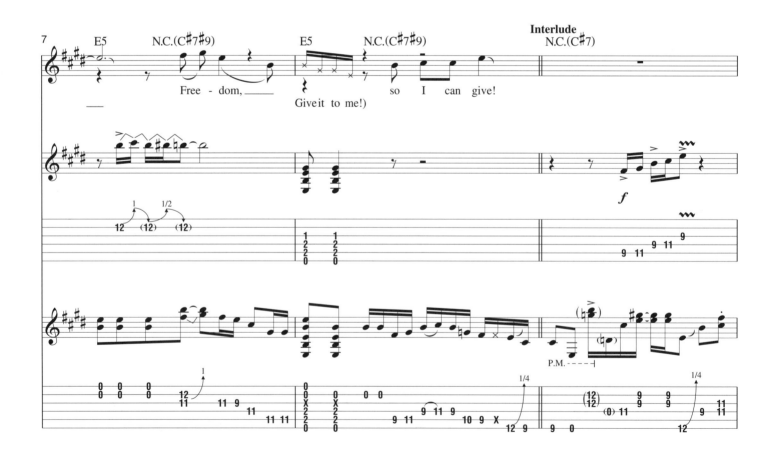

*T = Thumb on 6th string

Figure 25—Bridge

The eight-measure bridge temporarily tonicizes the IV chord (F♯) in what's basically another one-chord jam. Jimi creates a big, heavy sound here with a doubled guitar riff that answers a low power-chord assault on the first two eighth notes with a bluesy double-stop bend from the F♯ Dorian mode (F♯–G♯–A–B–C♯–D♯–E) on the "and" of beat 3.

Performance Tip: Jimi's tone here is perfect as usual—biting and aggressive. Use the bridge pickup and really dig in to get the appropriate tone.

Fig. 25

43 Full Band

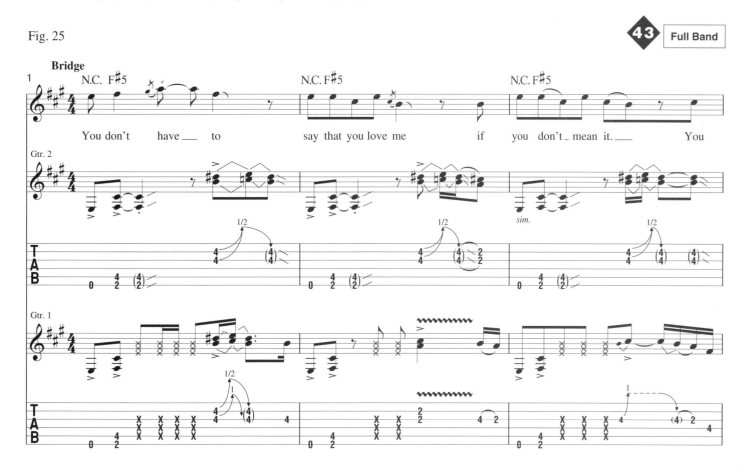

*Fade in w/ volume pedal or knob.

Figure 26—Guitar Solo

Jimi's sixteen-measure solo in this tune is all over the place. Considering the brevity of the section, it's amazing how many different approaches are covered. Based on an implied progression that moves F#–E–F# every four measures, the solo is neatly divided into basically two eight-measure sections. Gtr. 1 supports through the first eight with mostly double-stop and single-note riffs based off the F# Dorian mode. Gtr. 2 begins the solo with some snarling whole-step bends in the low register, resolving to the open low E string with the implied E change in measure 2. In measure 3 he whips out a syncopated lick from E minor pentatonic alternating the open low E string with a D–E hammer on string 4 that's treated to a generous amount of panning, to say the least. He moves up to fourteenth position with F#m pentatonic for the return to F# in measure 4 and remains there through measure 8.

Gtr. 1 takes the stage at measure 9 with a two-measure, syncopated riff based on the F# Mixolydian mode (F#–G#–A#–B–C#–D#–E) with an added chromatic B# note. Notice how the G# note on beat 3 of measure 10 functions as both the hip 9th of F# and the 3rd of the implied E harmony at that point. Gtr. 2 joins in at measure 11, harmonizing in 3rds. This is only a tease, though, as he quickly abandons the idea on beat 4 and fills out the rest of the phrase with percussive clicks. He resumes his soloing in measure 13 at the fourteenth-fret F# minor pentatonic box, but this time with a surprising switch to a clean tone. It actually sounds as if his guitar is plugged directly into the board. He remains in this position for the final four measures, tearing up the pentatonic box with sixteenth-note flurries and signature vibrato.

44	**Full Band**
	Slow Demo
45	Gtr. 2 meas. 3–4, 7–8, 14–16
	Gtr. 1 meas. 9–10

Fig. 26

Guitar Solo

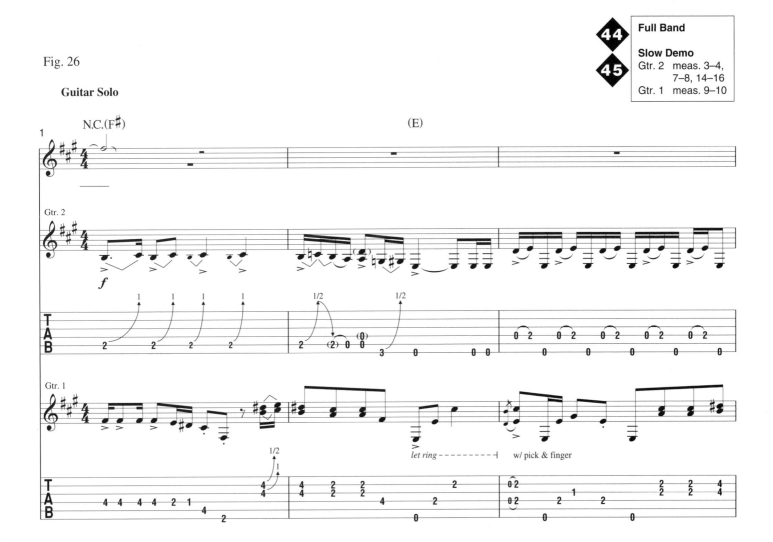

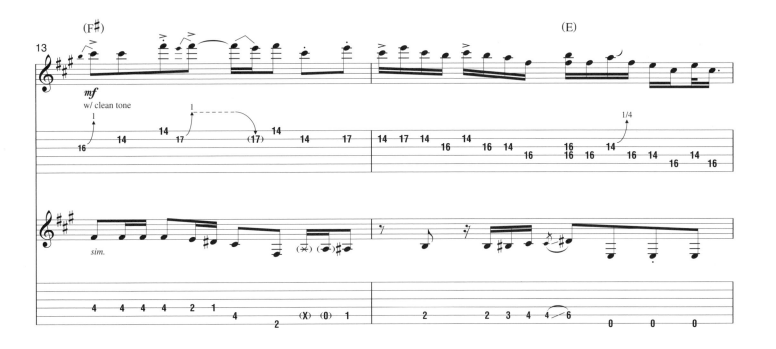

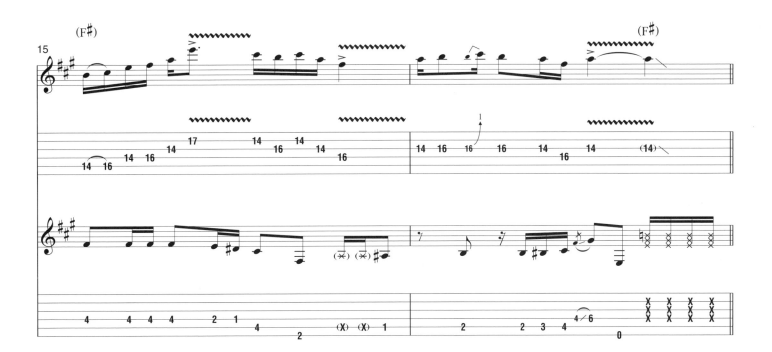

Figure 27—Outro Chorus and Outro

Things just keep getting funkier and funkier during the outro chorus. Hendrix brings back the funky interlude riff (Gtr. 1) for this chorus, expanding on it in beat 4 with a few high double-stop jabs. Gtr. 2 fills things out with percussive clicks, octave shapes, and funky double- and triple-stops from the C#m pentatonic scale. At measure 11 Hendrix borrows from himself with a stuttering, syncopated riff that's extremely similar to one in "Crosstown Traffic," even down to the vocal "do, do, do's." Gtr. 2 basically descends down the C#m pentatonic scale through the two-measure phrase, while Gtr. 1 descends through double stops from the C# Dorian mode.

For the outro, Hendrix pulls out all the stops, sequencing a descending Blues scale riff that alternates between 3/8 and 2/4 time signatures, moving down in whole steps. After four times through the sequence, a syncopated ensemble riff ensues that moves a C#9 voicing up by minor 3rds, eventually reaching the octave C#9 shape to finish things off. Phew!

Fig. 27

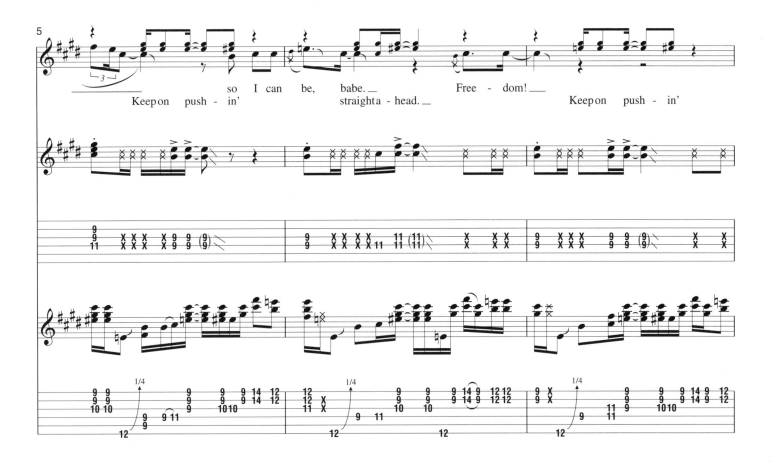

so I can be, babe. __ Free - dom! __

Keep on push - in' straight a - head. __ Keep on push - in'

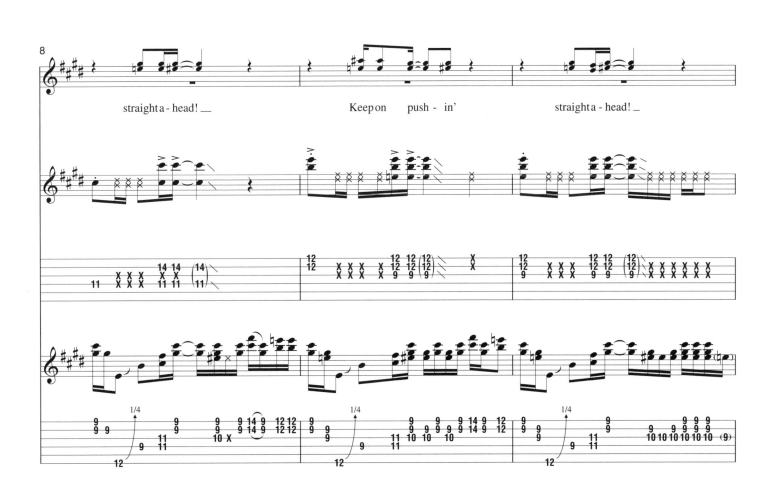

straight a - head! __

Keep on push - in' straight a - head! __

Keep on push - in'...
Do, do, do, do, do, do, do, do, do, do, do, do, do, do, do, do, do, do, do, do!)

HEY BABY (NEW RISING SUN)
(First Rays of the New Rising Sun, 1997)
Words and Music by Jimi Hendrix

Figure 28—Intro: Sections A–C

"Hey Baby (New Rising Sun)" features one of the longest intros in the Hendrix catalog. At 51 measures in length, it runs through several different tempos, keys, time signatures, and grooves before settling into anything. Hendrix begins with an unaccompanied guitar riff in which he uses several sixteenth-note chromatic-laced runs to connect E, C, and G chords. This is followed by a 6/4 measure where D, A, and E receive two beats each. Needless to say, it's pretty much impossible to determine what key, if any, we're in at this point.

At measure 5 (section B), the guitar and bass embark on another chromatically descending riff that seems to come to rest on a C chord in measure 6, but in the very next measure (5/4) we launch into another disorienting run in quarter-note triplets outlining G7/F. In measure 8, the drums join in for a final set of descending lines that seem to suggest an F Mixolydian mode (F–G–A–Bb–C–D–Eb), although the chord that finally arrives at the downbeat of measure 10 is Eb. This kicks off the odd chord progression of Eb–Bb, Db–G, Ab–A, Bb, which is then repeated, the only difference being the movement to C5 at the end of the final measure.

Section C kicks off with an F chord, and due to the previous C chord, this almost provides a sense of F major as the tonic. Jimi uses a two-beat scalar line to walk down to the following Bb chord, and the possibility of the F major tonic is strengthened, as the Bb sounds like a IV chord. However, that notion is immediately done away with, as we soon realize that this I–IV idea is being transposed and sequenced down in minor 3rds. A D5 chord is followed with a walk down through a D major scale to G, which is in turn followed by a B chord and major scale walkdown to E. The tempo then retards on the E, signaling that yet another change is coming.

Fig. 28

48 Full Band

Tune down 1/2 step:
(low to high) Eb-Ab-Db-Gb-Bb-Eb

A Intro

Slowly ♩ = 66

*E

Gtr. 1 (slight dist.)

C

mp   P.M.
w/ univibe
vibrato

slight P.M.

* Chord symbols reflect implied harmony.
** Let downstem notes ring where possible.

G

D

A

E

***T

Harm.

***T = Thumb on 6th string

Figure 29—Intro: Sections D–E

With the arrival of section D , we finally reach the actual key of the song: A minor. Hendrix kicks off the new groove, which is slightly faster, and introduces the two-measure Am–G–F–D5 progression that will serve as the basis for a good deal of the song. He decorates the chords with typical embellishments throughout, and the band joins him once again in measure 5.

At section E , Jimi begins to solo, accompanied only by the bass and drums. His lines here, based mostly off the A minor hexatonic scale (A–B–C–D–E–G) are slippery and somewhat reminiscent of Robby Krieger of the Doors. He gets much mileage out of the open position as well as the more standard fifth-fret A minor box . He also exploits the open high E and B strings often, creating wide interval leaps (measure 13) and dense clusters (measures 16 and 20).

The Blues scale is put to use in measures 17–20, and measure 19 contains the same pre-bent blue note bend lick that we saw in "Freedom" earlier. In measure 21 Hendrix lays into a sixteenth-note blues-approved move combining an E/G dyad on strings 3 and 2 with the open E string for a thick sound. This approach self destructs in the next measure into a chromatically-descending barre on the top three strings, signaling Jimi's return to rhythm guitar and his spoken inquiry, "Is the microphone on?"

49 Full Band

50 Slow Demo
Gtr. 1   meas. 17–20

Fig. 29

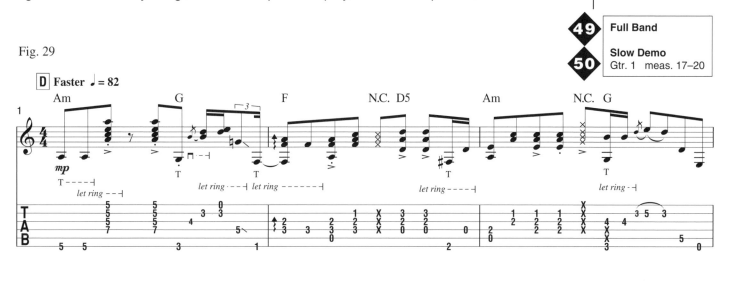

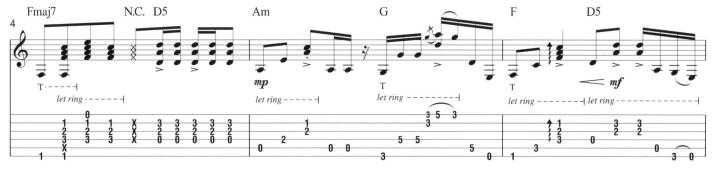

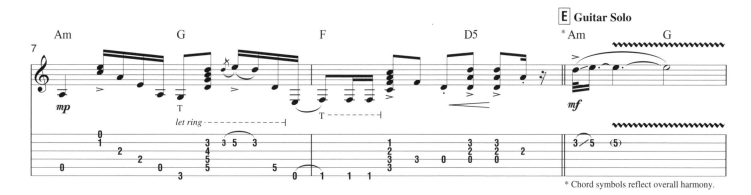

* Chord symbols reflect overall harmony.

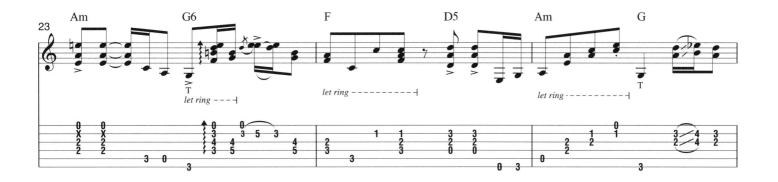

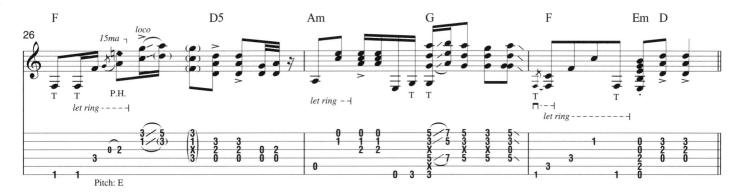

Figure 30—Chorus

The "New Sun" finally rises for the chorus, as we change to the parallel key of A major. The main section of the chorus is eight measures long, and each odd-numbered measure contains an A–C#5 progression. The even-numbered measures, however, receive two different treatments. Measures 2 and 6 follow a D chord on the downbeat with sixteenth-note octaves that descend chromatically from G♮ to F♮, while measures 4 and 8 answer the D chord with a colorful Gadd9 voicing in seventh position with the bass providing the root. Measure 4 follows this voicing with a nifty A major pentatonic riff in beats 3–4.

In measure 9 the chorus wraps up with a brief 6/8 chord progression of E–G–Bm–D, followed by a 2/4 extension of the D chord, which Hendrix treats in classic chord-melody style.

Performance Tip: When strumming the octave shapes, allow your first finger to damp the fifth string and third string, while your pinky damps the high E string.

Fig. 30

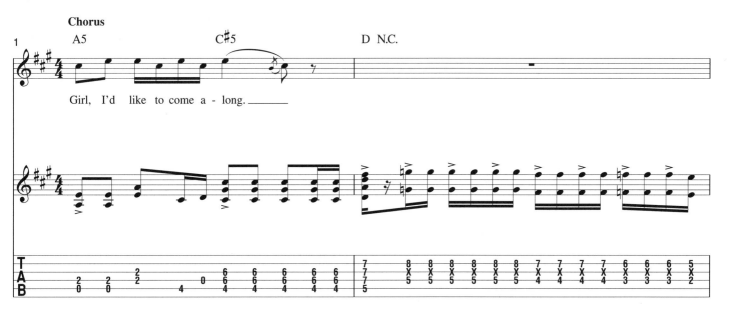

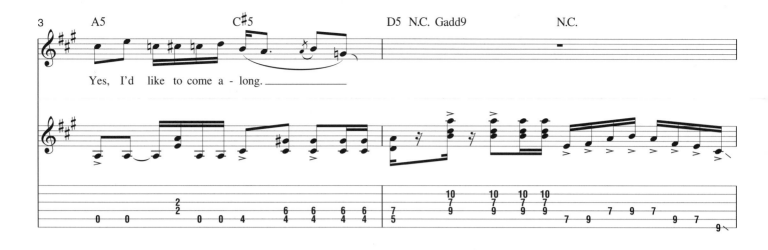

Yes, I'd like to come a-long.

"Would you like to come a-long?" she asked _ me. _

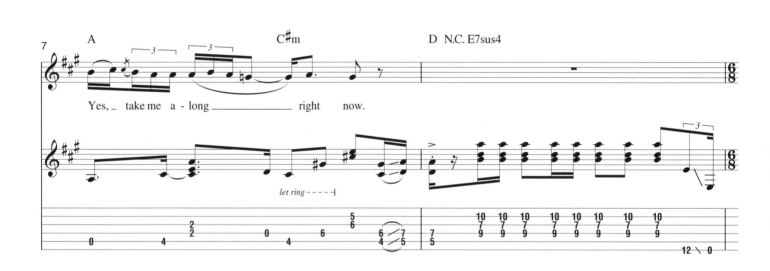

Yes, _ take me a-long _____ right now.

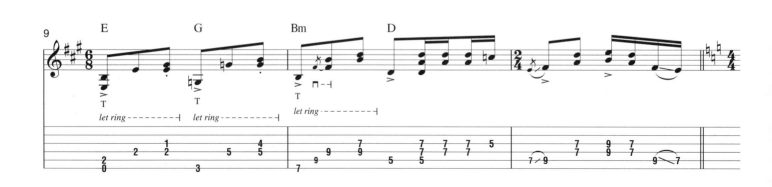

Figure 31—Interlude and Guitar Solo 2

Hendrix transposes an idea to each of the Am, G, and F chords for the four-measure interlude, arpeggiating the notes of a power chord to create a lopsided, somewhat clumsy-sounding riff. He begins his second solo by stringing together several bluesy phrases in measures 5–7 before grabbing the listener's attention on beat 1 of measure 8 with a D–F hammer on. Though the F is only one note (and the chord is in fact F at that point), the effect is still striking due to the overwhelming use of the pentatonic sound (and therefore *avoidance* of the F note) thus far.

Hendrix locks into the groove for measures 9–12 and delivers some spot-on pentatonic lines that include a few brief thirty-second-note pull-offs and a smooth position shift down the neck to bring the low open E string into the picture. In measure 13, he briefly moves into some high-register triple stops, sounding C, D, and E (!) triads for an ear-catching effect before returning to his open-position approach in measure 15. More slippery open-string legato lines follow, and he closes the solo with some rapid thirty-second-note picking in measures 19–20.

52 **Full Band**

53 **Slow Demo**
Gtr. 1   meas. 9–12, 15–20

Fig. 31

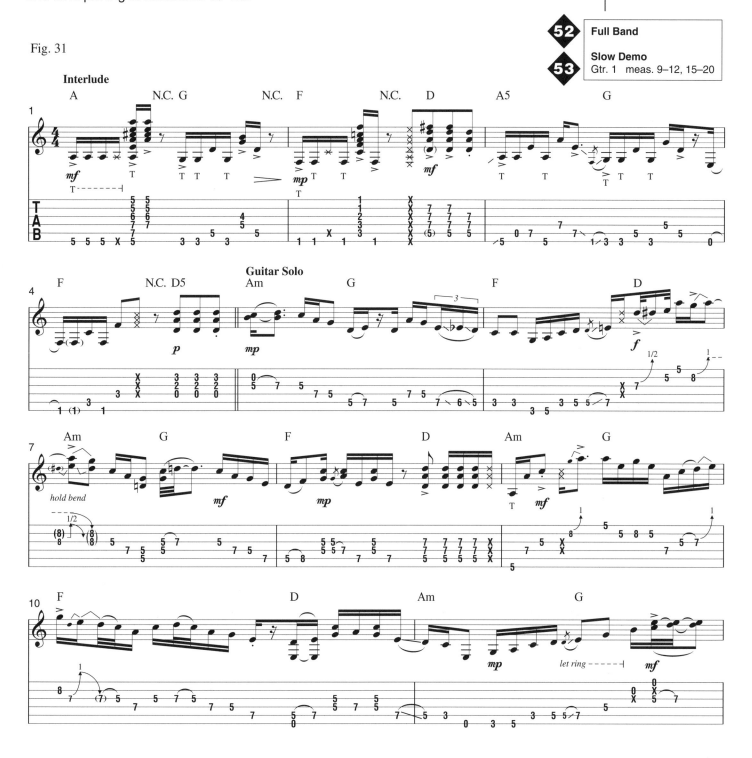

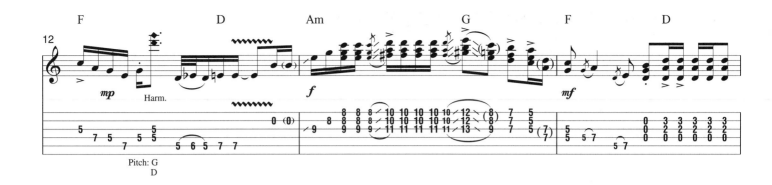

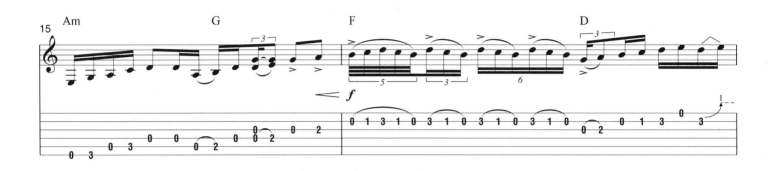

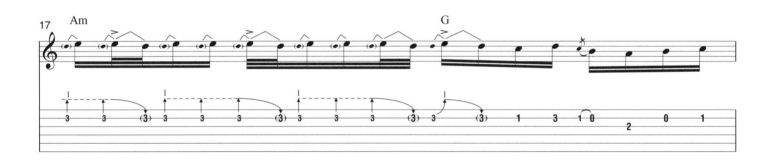

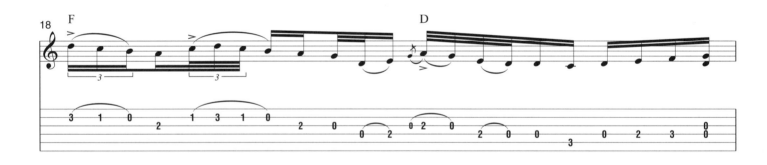

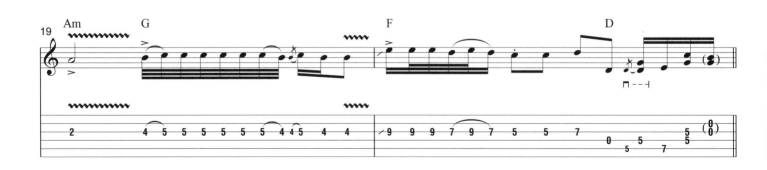

I DON'T LIVE TODAY
(*Are You Experienced*, 1967)
Words and Music by Jimi Hendrix

Recorded in February of 1967, "I Don't Live Today" appeared on *Are You Experienced* as one of the more straight-ahead, riff-driven tracks. Similar to "Freedom" (and in stark contrast to "Hey Baby (New Rising Sun)"), the song is harmonically as bare bones as it gets; it's basically a one-chord jam.

Figure 32—Intro and Verse

After two measures of drums, Hendrix enters with a two-measure honking, staccato riff based off a seventh-position B7 chord shape to get things under way. This is followed immediately by the riff that serves as the backbone for much of the song. Doubled by the bass, Gtr. 1 descends down the B minor pentatonic scale in eighth notes from the ♭7th (A) to the root, which is sustained across the next measure beneath the vocal phrases, treating the minor 3rd (D) to bluesy quarter- and half-step bends along the way. In measures 9 and 13 this riff is altered to end on the ♭7th (A) and 5th (F♯), respectively, creating a twelve-measure section that somewhat implies a 12-bar blues form.

Gtr. 2 enters in measure 7, contributing feedback swells on the notes B and F♯. This feedback increases in intensity throughout the second verse (not shown).

Performance Tip: Although the music calls for the thumb on the sixth string during the opening B7 riff, the first finger can just as easily be used if it's too tough to reach the high A note with your pinky.

Fig. 32

54 Full Band

55 Slow Demo
Gtr. 1 meas. 3–4

Figure 33—Chorus

The eight-measure chorus is basically a repeated four-measure phrase. Measures 1–3 and 5–7 open with two quarter-note accents. Gtr. 2 executes an oblique triple-stop bend from the B minor pentatonic box, while Gtr. 1 alternates between hammering out three-note Bm7 voicings and doubling Gtr. 2. For beats 3–4, Gtr. 1 walks chromatically in octaves from D to E, adding fuel to the frenzy. In measures 4 and 8, Gtr. 1 rounds out the phrase with a root–5th–♭7th eighth-note figure doubled by the bass.

Fig. 33

Figure 34—Guitar Solo

Hendrix kicks on the Octavia pedal for a sixteen-measure solo that basically takes place over a B pedal tone. While Gtr. 1 provides support (or countermelodies) with mostly octaves from the B Dorian mode, the only chord it actually plays is a B5 in measures 7–8, leaving things wide open for the solo.

Jimi takes advantage of this clean harmonic slate, slip-sliding around and drawing from both the B Dorian (B–C#–D–E–F#–G#–A) and Mixolydian (B–C#–D#–E–F#–G#–A) modes at some point. He begins in Dorian mode, accenting the colorful 9th (C#) in measures 3–4 and the bright major 6th (G#) in measures 5–6. With the presence of the D# he taps into the Mixolydian mode in measure 7, but quickly returns to the Dorian sound in measure 11. Measures 5, 10, 12–13, and 15–16 receive their fair share of tremolo bar antics, in typical Hendrix fashion.

Fig. 34

Figure 35—Outro (excerpt)

The outro begins with Jimi returning to the verse riff unaccompanied at a slightly faster tempo. Unlike the verse, however, the first measure of the riff is now repeated continuously in a steady stream of driving eighth notes. Gtr. 2 enters at measure 5 with a slow gliss up to the tonic B note, at which time Gtr. 1 begins to abandon the riff in favor of percussive clicks, eventually settling into Rhy. Fig. 1 at measure 9. Gtr. 2 continues treating sporadic notes from the B minor pentatonic scale with feedback and tremolo bar manipulation, joined eventually by Gtr. 4 in measure 11, to provide a sonic bed of sirens and wails over which Gtr. 3 begins to solo. With a half dirty tone, Gtr. 3 peels off some tough blues licks from the B minor pentatonic box in seventh position. Note the gorgeous vibrato applied to the D note in measure 11—a typical Hendrix technique that he made sound so effortless. He briefly references the B Dorian mode in measure 14 with the presence of the 6th (G♯) and gives another lesson in vibrato in measures 15 and 17. He finishes up in measures 24–25 with a run up and down the B minor pentatonic box, including the blues note (F♮) on the way down and a minor/major 3rd bend at the end.

Fig. 35

59 Full Band

60 Slow Demo
Gtr. 3 meas. 14, 21, 24–25

Outro
In time ♩ = 132

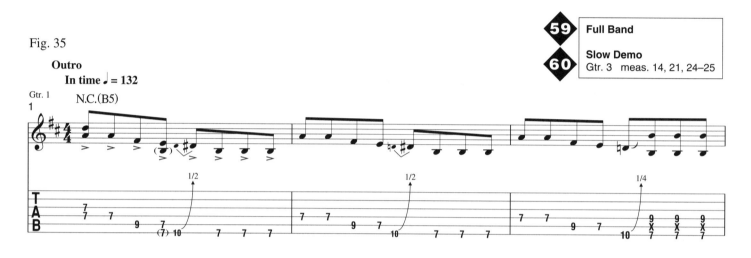

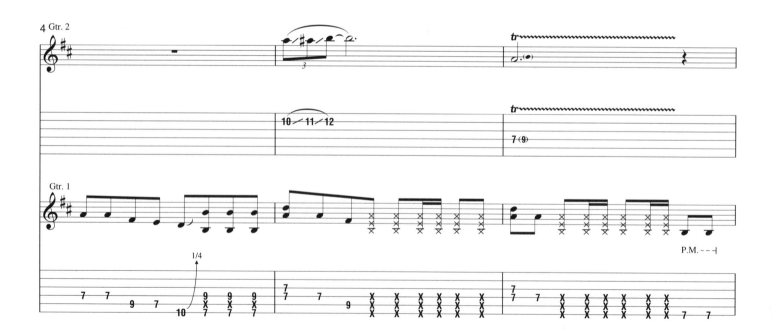

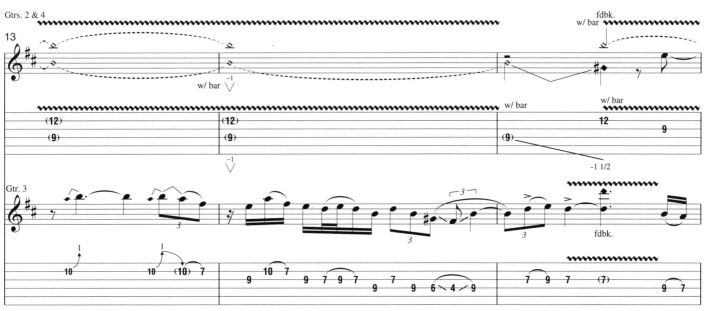

MACHINE GUN
(*Band of Gypsys*, 1970)
Words and Music by Jimi Hendrix

There are certainly many things that separate Hendrix from the masses when it comes to his guitar playing, and one of those is his innate ability to simply make the guitar *speak*—to make the guitar say something unmistakable in its emotional delivery. This is something that cannot be attributed to merely one aspect. Rather, it is the combined result of practically all the aspects of playing; his tone, touch, note choice, rhythmic phrasing and conception, and the musical context all come into play. "Machine Gun" is a prime example of this ability. Recorded at the New Year's Eve concerts from the Fillmore East, New York, in 1969, the tune is simply one of the most riveting pieces of live guitar work in history.

Figure 36—Intro

"Machine Gun" is essentially a one-chord jam in Jimi's favorite key of E. It's very similar to "Voodoo Child" in structure, and it begins the same way with Hendrix playing unaccompanied riffs from E minor pentatonic (E–G–A–B–D). Mixing open strings with the twelfth-position box, Jimi begins by filling the gaps around an A–G motive with various percussive clicks, low open E string stabs, and connective runs through Em pentatonic. The targeted G melody note is treated to gorgeous Hendrix vibrato each time.

At measure 5, he begins to hint at the namesake "machine gun" technique by rattling off thirty-second-note percussive strokes on beat 1 followed by slight variations on the A–G melodic theme that introduce some whole-step bends. Billy Cox creeps in on bass in measure 6, and Jimi pulls off a beautifully fluid line in measure 7 that kicks off with a high D bent up to E and cascades down to an E–D pull-off on string 4 in a rhapsodic rhythm.

The drums enter at measure 9, doubling Jimi's percussive thirty-second notes, and Jimi and Billy lock in during beats 2–4 with the intro theme proper built from the E Blues scale. After four statements of this theme, the band settle into a groove at measure 13, and Jimi peels off a few classic, open-position blues licks laced with trills. He rounds out the twenty-four-measure intro with numerous highlights: quick, bluesy pentatonic runs (measures 15–17), thick wide vibrato (measures 17–18, 21), and slippery legato phrasing (measures 19–21). And this is just the intro!

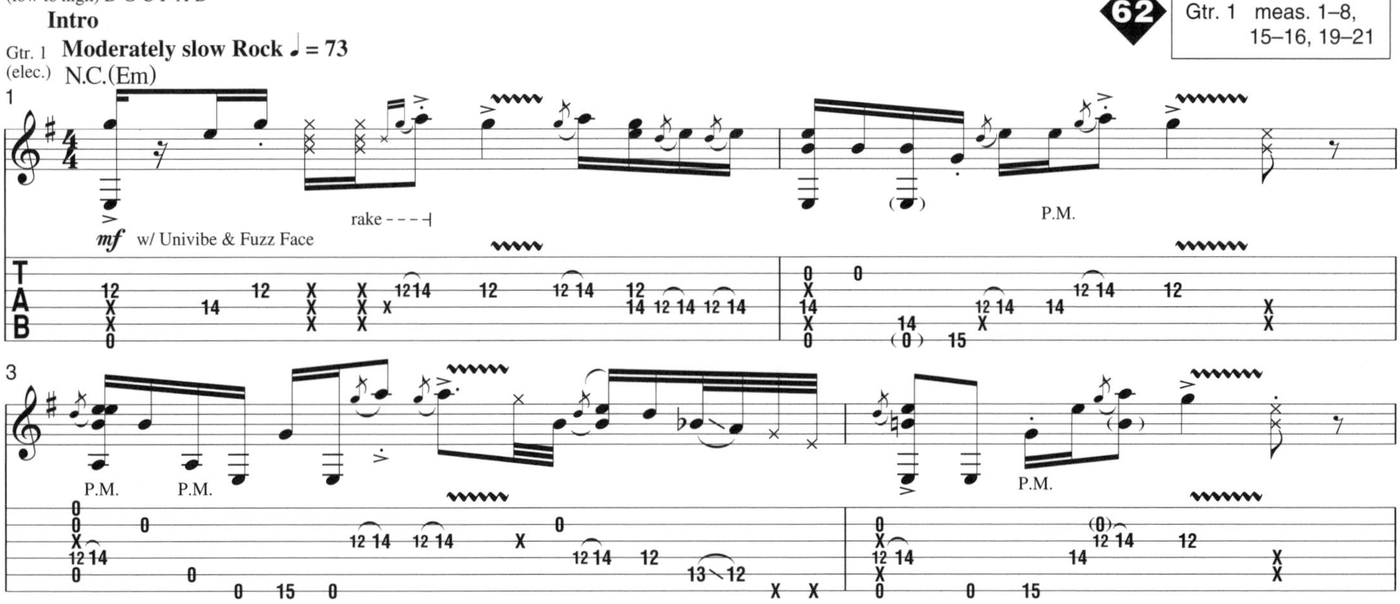

Note: Hendrix is tuned down a whole step for this song instead of the usual half step.

61 Full Band

62 Slow Demo
Gtr. 1 meas. 1–8, 15–16, 19–21

Fig. 36

Tune down 1 step:
(low to high) D-G-C-F-A-D

* T = Thumb on 6th string

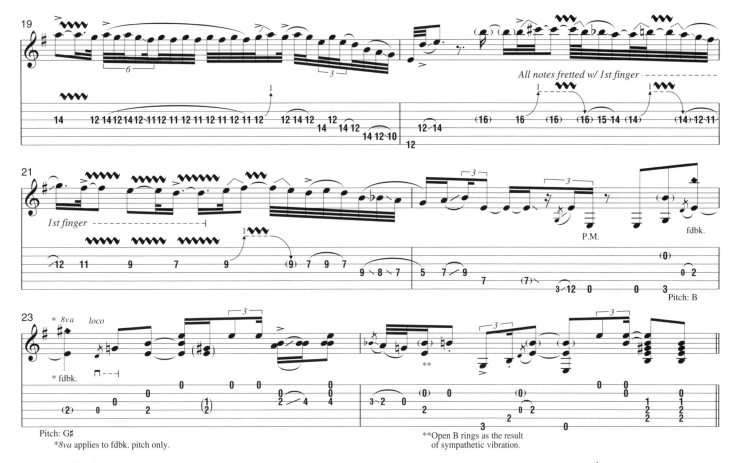

Figure 37—Verse 1

Jimi approaches the first verse of "Machine Gun" much like "Voodoo Child," often doubling the vocal melody with the guitar and filling in the holes with bluesy, open-position fills. At some points, this is done with impressive exactness, as in measure 3, while other times it's more of an approximation, as in measure 8. In measures 4 and 5 we see the bluesy 6th interval of D/B played on strings 5 and 3—a favorite of Hendrix's that can be heard in similar songs in the key of E, such as "Hey Joe" and "Hear My Train a Comin'."

In measures 9 and 10 Hendrix sneaks out a few high, wailing G notes bent a whole step to A and treated to some heavy vibrato for a dramatic effect. Jimi, much like Stevie Ray Vaughan after him, possessed the ability to move effortlessly between the twelfth-fret box and the open-position E minor pentatonic on a dime as demonstrated with these phrases. In measure 11 Jimi pulls off an ultra-cool lick in which he repeatedly bends and releases the D note a whole step in a lazy, swung sixteenth-note rhythm that just oozes groove.

Fig. 37

63 Full Band

64 Slow Demo
Gtr. 1 meas. 3–6, 7–10

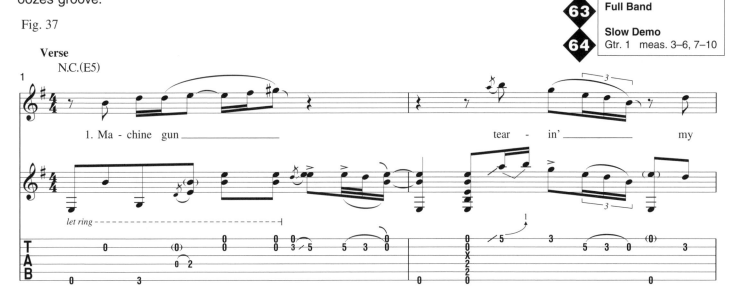

bod - y _____ all a - part. _____

Pitch: G#

Ma - chine gun, _____ yeah,

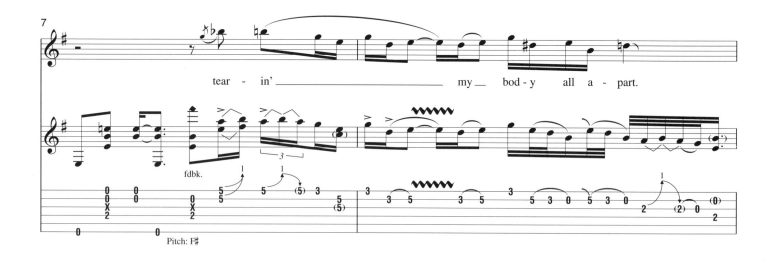

tear - in' _____ my _ bod - y all a - part.

Pitch: F#

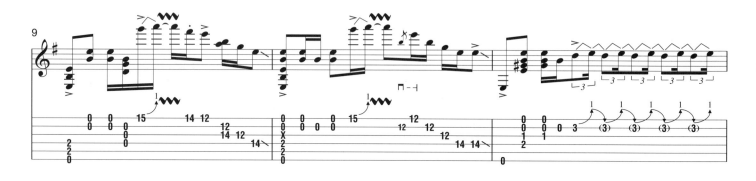

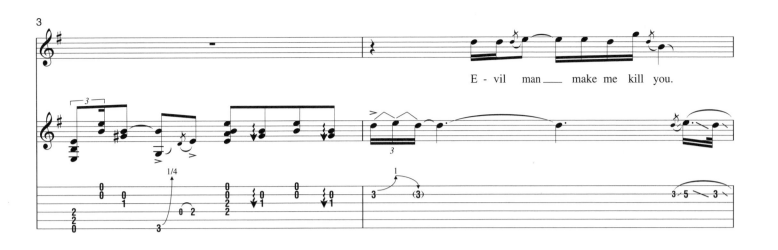

E - vil man___ make me kill you.

E - vil man make you kill me.   E - vil___ man___ make___ me kill you,___

e - ven though___ we're on - ly fam-'lies___ a - part.___

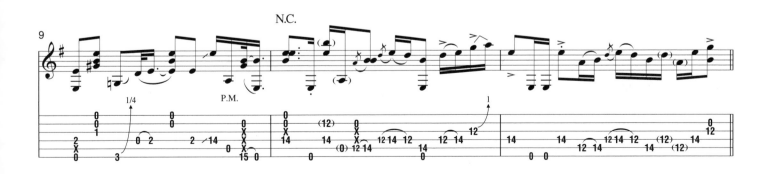

N.C.

Figure 38—Verse 2

For the second verse, Hendrix moves up exclusively to the twelfth-fret box position and continues his method of doubling some of his vocal lines while filling in the gaps. This "filling in" of the gaps, however, consists of some stellar phrasing. Measure 4 contains some beautiful vibrato on both unbent (G) and bent notes (D), while measure 5 begins with a virtuosic thirty-second-note descending line through E minor pentatonic. Speaking of vibrato, the end of measure 9 contains some of the most wicked demonstrations you're likely to ever hear.

The lick at the end of measure 5 demonstrates that, with a unique rhythmic approach, the simple act of ascending through a minor pentatonic scale can still sound fresh and alive. More brilliance can be found in measures 11–13, where he combines sixteenth notes, sixteenth-note triplets, and thirty-second notes together in several unique and catchy rhythms. Don't miss the syncopated lick in beats 3–4 of measure 13 where he repeats a pattern of six notes in straight thirty-second notes in a crammed pentatonic barrage.

65	**Full Band**
66	**Slow Demo**
	Gtr. 1 meas. 5–6, 10–13

Fig. 38

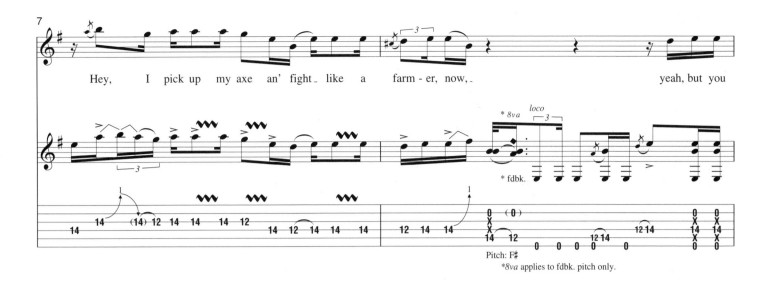

Hey, I pick up my axe an' fight like a farm-er, now,_ yeah, but you

*8va applies to fdbk. pitch only.

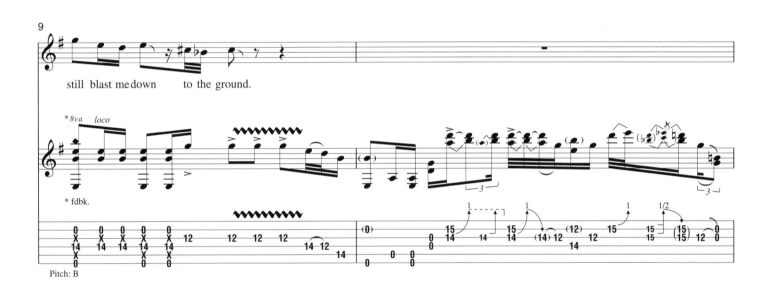

still blast me down to the ground.

Pitch: B

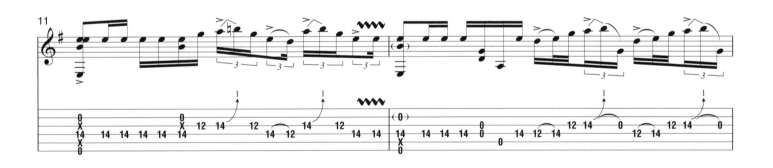

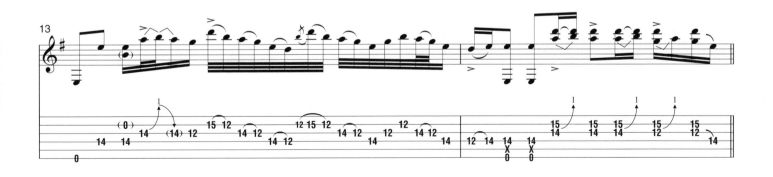

Figure 39—Guitar Solo

There are many instances in popular culture, including sports, art, music, etc., when we can point to one specific event that transcends the constraints of what we normally consider within the realm of human achievement. In sports, for example, we have Babe Ruth "calling his shot" in the World Series of 1932, Franco Harris's "immaculate reception," the 1980 U.S. hockey team beating Russia to win the gold, etc. In music, we guitar players have Jimi's solo in "Machine Gun." In perhaps the most breathtaking beginning of any guitar solo in history, Jimi bends the seventeenth-fret A note on string 1 up a whole step to B, and something magical happens. "The note" simply comes *alive*, sustaining for nearly two full measures before Hendrix dips slightly with the bar and strikes it again at the beginning of measure 3, achieving the same effect.

Analyzing this solo almost seems absurd, as just about every note Jimi touches throughout its entirety turns to gold. And at seventy-one measures in length, that's saying something. The highlights are far too many to cover in this volume, but we'll touch upon a few that simply can't be ignored. Throughout the solo, Jimi seems to create his own vocabulary of string-bending licks, accessing unexpected or in-between notes in a way that simply defies analysis. See measures 5, 6, 9, 13, 34, and 35 for a few examples. Hendrix lets loose often with rapid-fire repetitive licks that give new meaning to the term "effortless," as heard in measures 7–8, 16–17, and 57–60 in particular.

Jimi's Strat takes plenty of tremolo bar abuse throughout the solo as well. In measure 19, he embarks on a six-measure trill between a high B and D to which he adds vibrato, dips, dives, and peaks with the bar. In measure 42 Jimi applies a bar dive to several long, sustained bent notes, all the while manipulating the speed of the Univibe pedal for a siren-like effect. Besides the more drastic effects, Jimi also uses the bar occasionally to apply vibrato at several points, as in measures 37 and 66. Jimi rounds out this epic by first tuning his low E string (measure 68) and then joining Billy Cox for an E minor pentatonic riff in fifth and seventh position.

As mentioned earlier, this entire solo is magical; there are no dull moments. If there's ever an "essential listening" list of guitar solos compiled that doesn't feature this song within the top five slots, a severe musical crime will have been committed.

67 Full Band

68 Slow Demo
Gtr. 1   meas. 6–10, 15–18, 27–33, 47–51, 57–64

Fig. 39

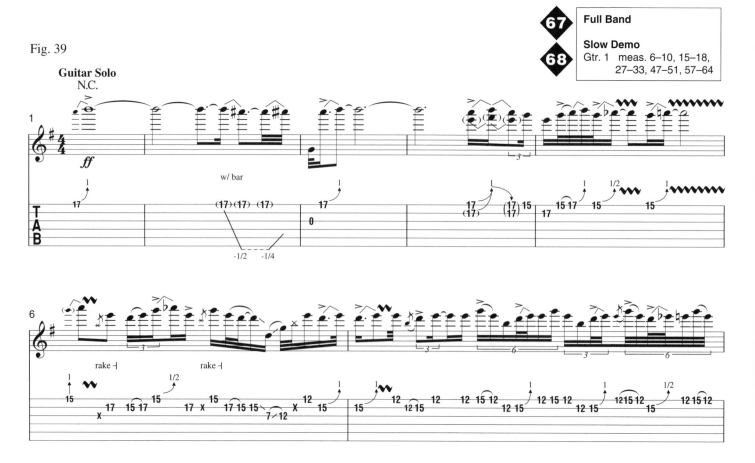

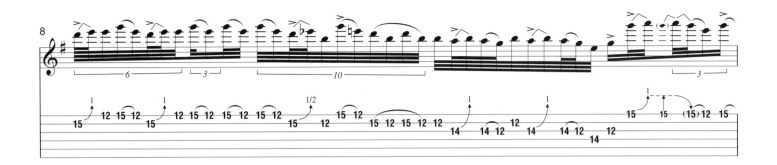

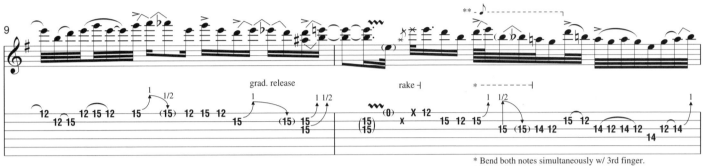

* Bend both notes simultaneously w/ 3rd finger.
** Played behind the beat.

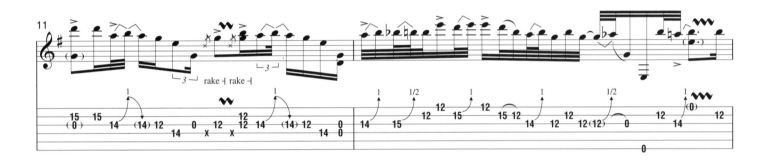

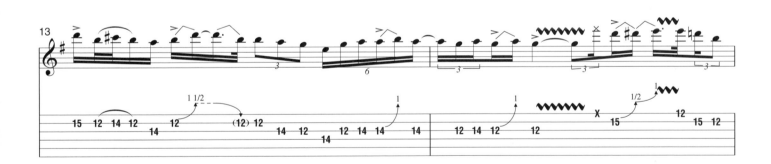

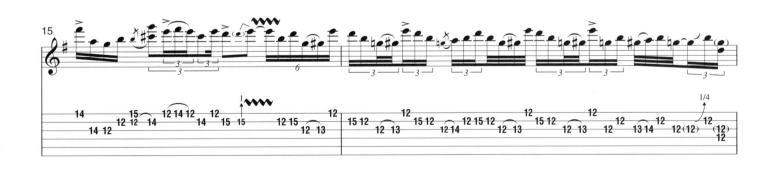

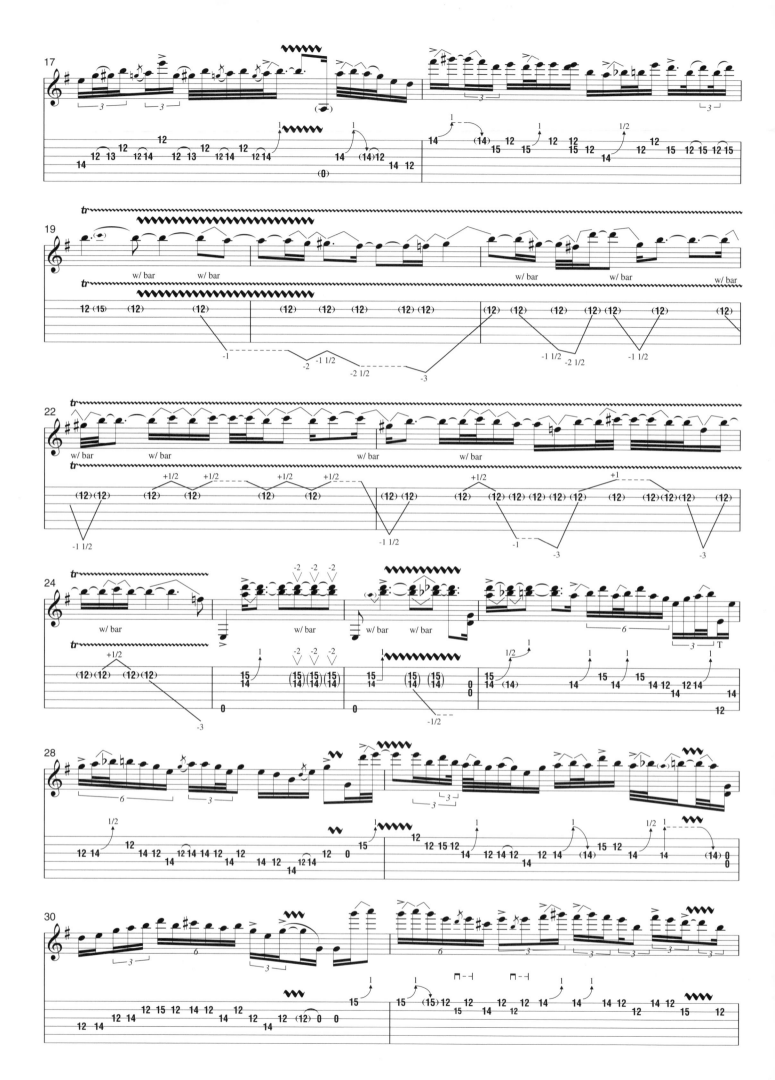

STAR SPANGLED BANNER (INSTRUMENTAL)
(*Woodstock*, 1969)
Adaptation by Jimi Hendrix

As much as Woodstock is romanticized by musical fans, the musicians that performed there often tell a different story. The sound was simply awful onstage as well as off, and equipment problems were too many to name. The festival was so rife with technical difficulties that by the time Hendrix went on, they were over ten hours behind schedule. Hendrix was reportedly very nervous about the show, as friend Leslie Aday remembers: "As we sat there, he seemed very nervous and didn't think he could pull it off. He didn't feel the band knew the songs well enough or had enough rehearsal." History, of course, would prove him wrong.

Jimi had made the national anthem a part of his live show for over a year prior to Woodstock; he even allegedly received threats in Dallas about performing his rendition. So there was some question as to whether it should be performed at the festival. It turned out to be, unquestionably, *the* definitive performance. As the sun rose on August 18, 1969, Jimi performed quite possibly the most famous (and controversial) version of the "Star Spangled Banner" ever.

Figure 40—Section A

Hendrix begins the anthem in fairly harmless fashion. He plays the melody mostly in open position (key of E) with the Fuzz Face and Univibe pedals engaged for a thick, wavering tone. As is often the case with Jimi's tone, it's prone to feedback, and there are plenty of sweet, heavenly tones created here as a result.

Hendrix dresses up the melody throughout with melodic turns (measures 6, 13, and 18), trills (measure 12), and an extended legato scalar flurry (measure 15). He also makes use of bends (measures 6, 14, 16, and 18) to scoop into notes, invoking a vocal quality.

Fig. 40

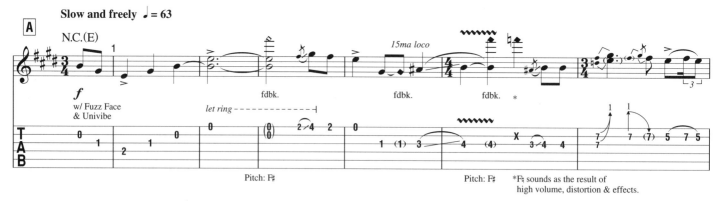

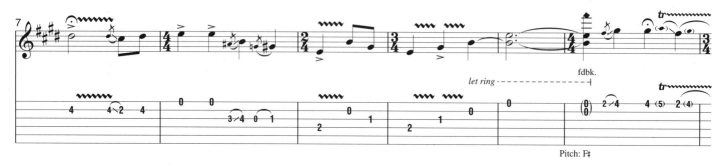

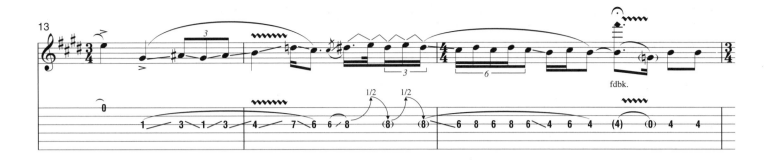

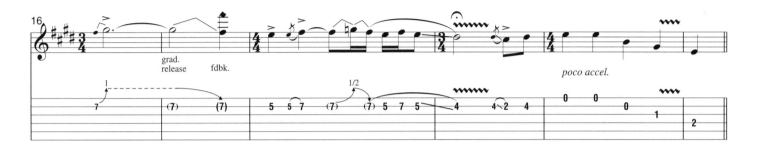

Figure 41—Section B

Jimi kicks on the wah wah for "And the rockets red glare..." and then lets loose. Applying radical tremolo bar maneuvers to a series of high bends, open strings, tremolo-picked triple stops, and feedback, he paints a picture of war. The effect is dramatic and shocking, to say the least, and was considered by many as outright blasphemy. Many others, however, found it to be a profound statement—a wakeup call that linked the audience to what was happening in Vietnam.

Hendrix quickly and suddenly brings his instrument back under control for "the bombs bursting in air..." and embarks upon another soundscape. He opens this one with the most "evil" of all intervals, the tritone, hammering alternating B♭ and E notes. He then moves on to full chords, hammering an E♭ chord shape at fret 8 and pulling off to the open G chord a minor 6th away. The open strings are then treated to some severe tremolo bar abuse, and the mayhem ensues as before. After Hendrix states the "gave proof through the night that our flag was still there" melody, he takes another type of liberty with the tune, sounding out the first few measures of the "Taps" bugle call.

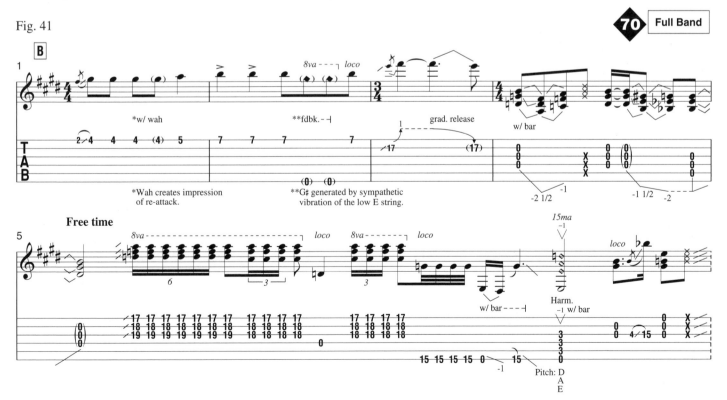

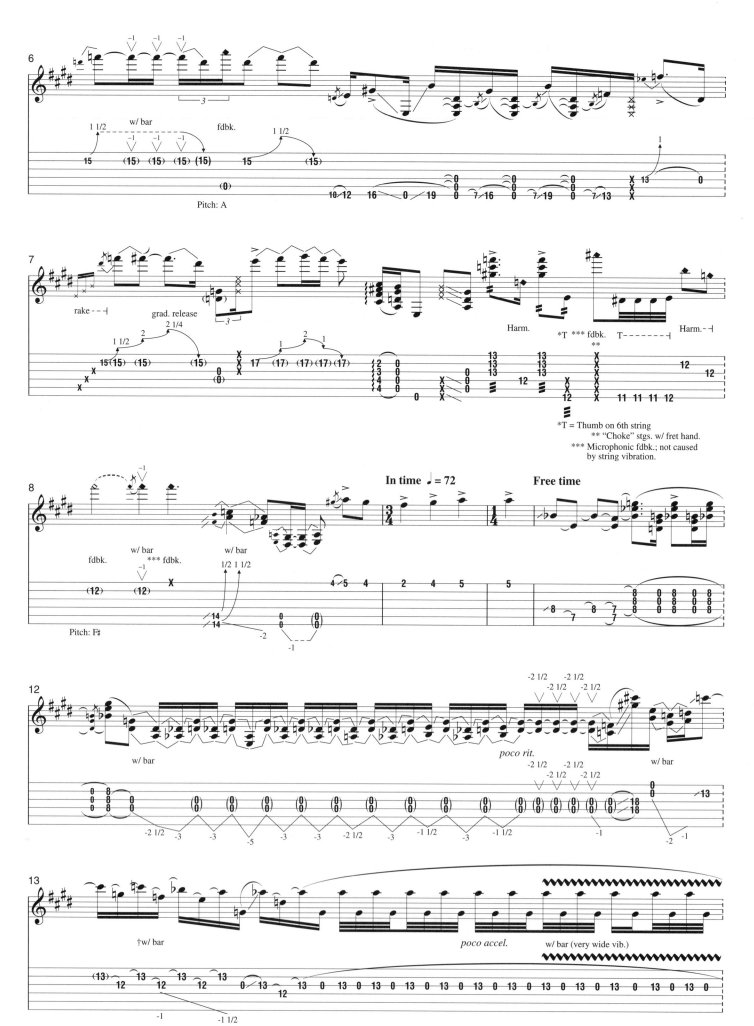

*T = Thumb on 6th string
** "Choke" stgs. w/ fret hand.
*** Microphonic fdbk.; not caused
by string vibration.

†Depress bar while "hammering-on from nowhere."

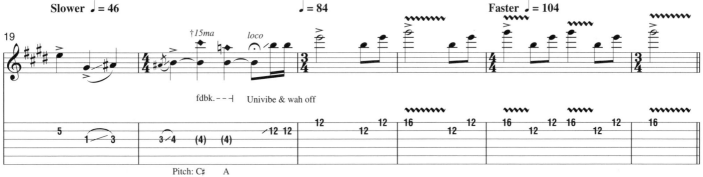

Figure 42—Section C

Hendrix handles the final section similar to the way he began the tune, sticking fairly close to the melody, but with the occasional diversion. In measures 5–9 he allows a sustained D♯ note to feed back, egging it on with tremolo bar dips of increasing intensity. He then kicks back on the wah for the "land of the free" line, allowing the high B note to enter the heavenly feedback realm and following it with a brief open-string divebomb with the bar. After finishing the melody with a few melodic embellishments, he kicks into a dramatic ascending chord finale of A–C–D–E5 and closes a chapter of pop culture history.

Fig. 42

71 Full Band

STONE FREE
(*Are You Experienced*, 1967)
Words and Music by Jimi Hendrix

Written as a B-side to the "Hey Joe" single in October of 1966, "Stone Free" was Hendrix's first composition—not too shabby for the first go-round! With lyrics aimed at the critics who didn't approve of Jimi's eccentric behaviors and style, the tune is filled with classic Hendrix riffs and recorded with minimal instrumentation; one guitar part carries the entire song. Interestingly, this song is performed in standard tuning, as opposed to Jimi's normal practice of tuning down a half step.

Figure 43—Intro

Jimi starts the song unaccompanied with two harmonic chimes (treated to some vibrato via the tremolo bar), joined shortly in measure 2 by bassist Noel Redding with a steady bass-line countoff to get the tune under way. The drums join in at measure 3 for the main riff, a low-register, palm-muted, eight-note line from the E minor pentatonic scale (E–G–A–B–D), interrupted with the occasional E7#9 chord stab. This chord would of course come to be known as the "Purple Haze" chord after that song's immense success. Jimi's tone is clean and fat here, with no hint of distortion at all.

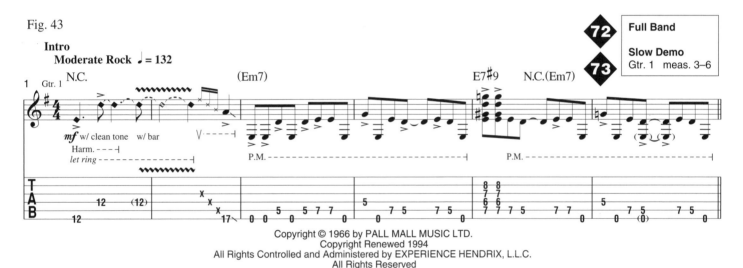

Figure 44—Verse and Pre-Chorus

The verse begins with the same riff as the intro, which continues through measure 8. At measure 9, the harmony moves to A7#9, and Jimi essentially transposes the riff up a 4th for the new chord. Since the tune is in the key of E, this move is very simple, allowing the open fifth string to be used in place of the open E. The riff is fingered the exact same way, only a string higher. The only exception to this is the 7#9 voicing, which differs by one fret. Jimi throws in a sassy blues fill in measure 12 from the Am pentatonic scale (A–C–D–E–G) in between vocal phrases.

At measure 13, we move back down to the E7#9 riff. At this point, the tune sounds like a double-length 12-bar blues form, and we expect to hear a V chord soon. Jimi finishes off the verse with an aggressive double-stop fill in seventh position at measure 16, and we then realize that the tune does not follow the 12-bar form.

The pre-chorus begins at measure 17 with what sounds somewhat like a key change to A. Jimi plants himself at the fifth-fret A barre chord shape and riffs ferociously through double stops from the A Dorian mode (A–B–C–D–E–F#–G), mixing in single-note runs from the A minor pentatonic scale and adding muscular vibrato. He moves to an A7#9 voicing in measures 23–24, heightening the tension for the approaching chorus.

Fig. 44

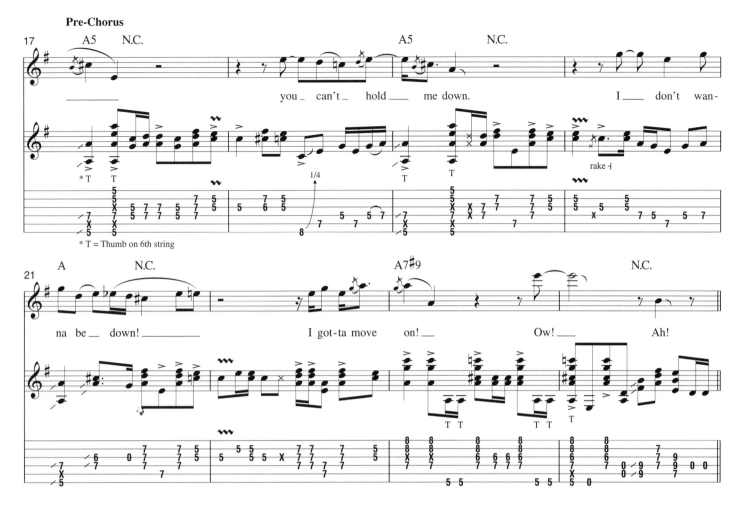

Figure 45—Chorus

The chorus changes keys to D major, and Jimi continues his riffing assault. Beginning in fifth position with a D barre chord shape, he alternates barring his third and first fingers to access alternating D and C chord shapes, respectively, on strings 4, 3, and 2. At measure 4, he rounds out the first phrase of the chorus with a move up to tenth position where he peels off a wicked double-stop fill in the D minor pentatonic box.

Hendrix remains in tenth position for the second half of the chorus, following D major chords on beat 1 with more tough minor pentatonic fills for the rest of the measure. At measure 7, Jimi applies full, six-string barre chord shapes to a new progression of C–A, dressing up each chord with a 9th on the top string via the pinky. He closes out the chorus with a sustained A chord, which he treats to a slight quarter-step rise and fall with the tremolo bar.

Performance Tip: In order to access the 9ths on the C and A chords, fretting the sixth string with your thumb is almost a must.

76 ◆ **Full Band**

77 ◆ **Slow Demo**
Gtr. 1 meas. 3–6

Fig. 45

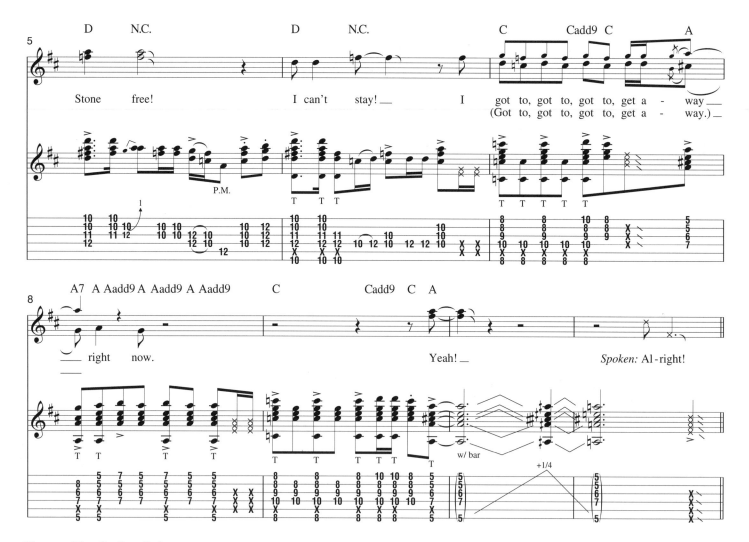

Figure 46—Guitar Solo

On the original recording, Jimi prefaces the solo with the exclamation, "Turn me loose, baby!" And he does indeed get turned loose. Stomping on the Fuzz Face, Jimi turns up the heat, working predominantly out of the A minor pentatonic scale. Though the solo is basically a one-chord jam in A, Jimi manages to keep things from getting stagnant, to say the least.

Right off the bat, we're given a serious slap in the face with a blues lick in measure 1 that's wrapped up with some *serious* vibrato. Jimi blazes up and down the pentatonic scale box in measures 3–4, covering the range of a 5th. He alludes briefly to the A minor hexatonic scale (A–B–C–D–E–G) in measures 3, 8, 9 (with a two-step bend from G), and 10 (with a whole-step bend from A). Jimi pivots high E and G notes against the open high E string in measures 9–10 in a frantic barrage and brings things to a close with a hard-groovin' line in measures 13–14, eventually wrapping up the section in the final two measures by banging out A7♯9 chords. Ow!

78 Full Band

79 Slow Demo
Gtr. 1

Fig. 46

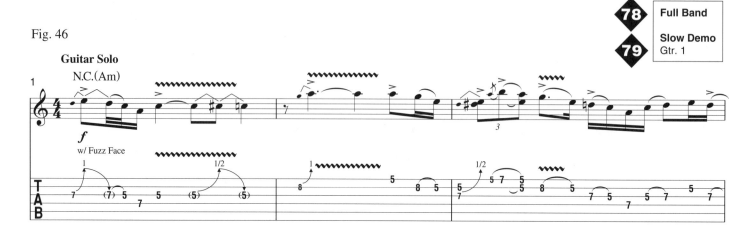

Figure 47—Chorus 3 and Outro

The third chorus is extended, and Jimi uses various ideas to keep the section fresh. In measures 2–3 and 4–6 he stabs at the low C note on string 6 with the pinky in between double and triple stops of C and D chords above. Every fourth measure (4, 8, 12, and 16) the whole band plays a syncopated ensemble riff that climbs chromatically from F♯ up to A on the upbeats, injecting new energy into each new four-measure phrase.

At measure 20, seemingly out of the blue, the outro begins with a Fuzz-Faced F5 chord and a tempo increase to 160 bpm. After an F octave is dipped with the bar, the strange section ends as quickly as it began with an abrupt fadeout.

Fig. 47

Chorus

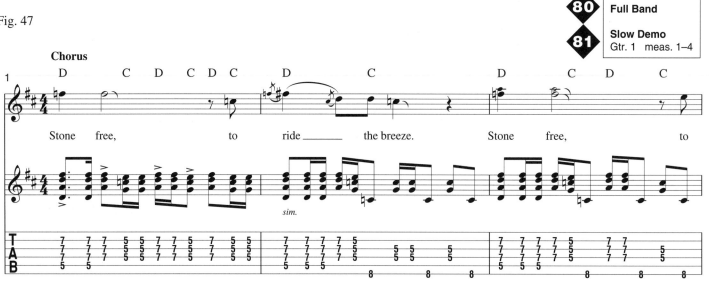

Stone free, to ride _____ the breeze. Stone free, to

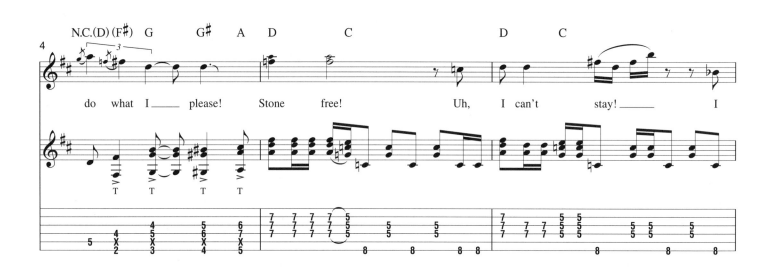

do what I _____ please! Stone free! Uh, I can't stay! _____ I

got to, got to, got to get a - way! I'm
(Stone free!) (Stone free!)

THIRD STONE FROM THE SUN

(*Are You Experienced*, 1967)

Words and Music by Jimi Hendrix

Appearing on the monumental debut album *Are You Experienced*, "Third Stone from the Sun" took listeners on a journey the likes of which they had never "experienced" before. Amazingly, the basic tracks for the song were wrapped up in one take in December, 1966, at CBS studios in London. Beautiful guitar work, catchy melodies, otherworldly noises, infectious mellow grooves, and tough, bluesy solos all somehow reside side by side in this track.

Figure 48—Intro and Interlude

The song opens with a straight eighth-note bass figure against a jazzy double-time swing feel by the drums over which Jimi plays the sparse, beautiful voicings of E6 and D6 with a lush clean tone, implying an E Mixolydian tonality (E–F♯–G♯–A–B–C♯–D). He then joins the bass line with a rolling eighth-note figure in measures 5–8 that pits a D5 shape over the open low E string. The mood darkens in measures 9–12 as Hendrix uses the open high E string as a drone against double stops and single notes on strings 2 and 3, creating a beautiful, dense melody derived from the E Dorian mode (E–F♯–G–A–B–C♯–D). This is a beautiful example of modal mixture, a device that Hendrix commonly employs in his songs in which chords from the major and parallel minor mode are both used (see "Angel"). The intro wraps up in measures 13–16 with an abbreviated return to the E6–D6 progression and the rolling D5/E figure.

For the brief four-measure interlude, the mode shifts to minor again. This time, however, the melody is built from the E natural minor scale (E–F♯–G–A–B–C–D) and is played on the G string against the open B and E strings as drones. This results in several dense clusters and unison notes for a unique, somewhat sitar-like sound. Jimi continues to use the high E string as a drone through the bluesy riff in measure 20 to close out the section.

Fig. 48

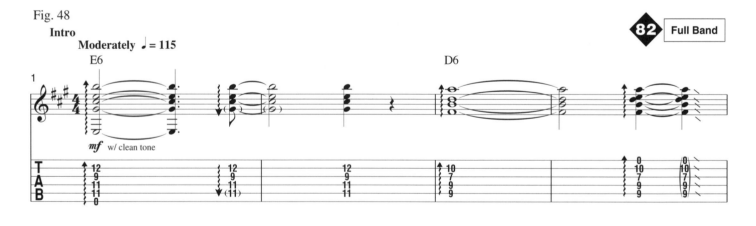

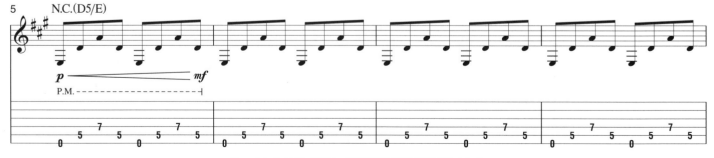

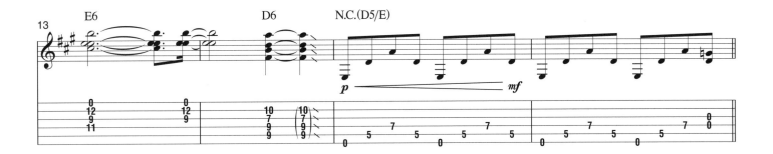

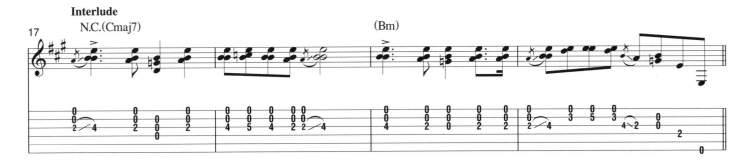

Figure 49—Theme, Interlude, and Guitar Solo

Drummer Mitch Mitchell switches to a more standard light rock beat for the theme. Drawing again from the E Mixolydian mode, Hendrix articulates the gorgeous theme in octaves against Redding's hypnotic bass line. He employs the bar throughout for vibrato (measures 4, 5–6, 11–12, 13–14, and 16) and rhythmic dips (measures 7, 9–10, 15, and 17–18).

The interlude is the same as the previous with the exception of the final measure, where Hendrix jumps mid-phrase up to the twelfth position E minor pentatonic box with a bluesy double-stop line to preface his solo.

At measure 23 Hendrix takes a brief, four-measure solo from the E minor pentatonic box at fret 12. Beginning with what would become a classic Hendrix move, he answers an open low E string stab with a D note at fret 15 of the second string bent up to E. This same type of lick can be heard in his classic ballad "Little Wing."

Fig. 49

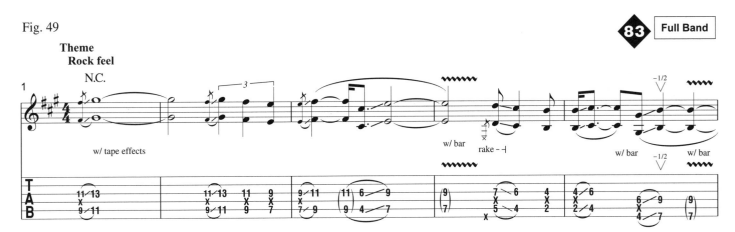

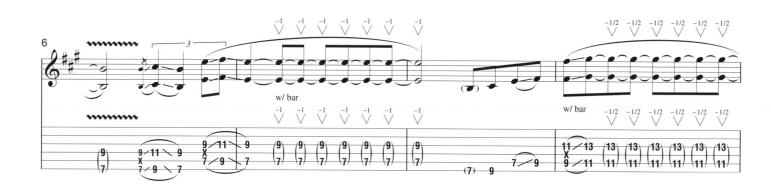

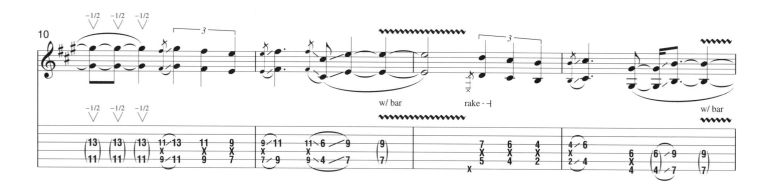

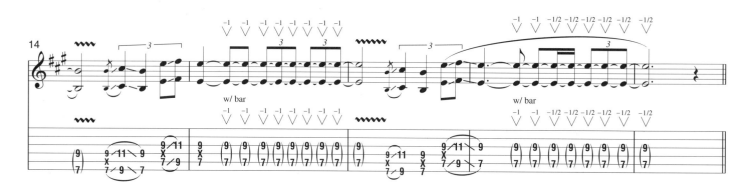

Interlude

Guitar Solo

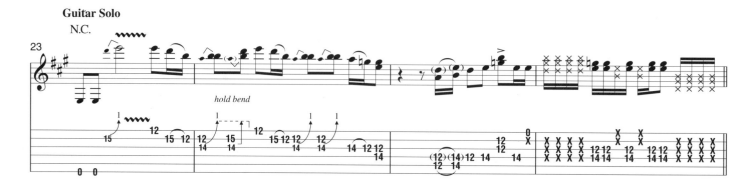

Figure 50—Verse

The verse maintains some of the energy gained during the guitar solo, but Hendrix supports his otherworldly address to the planet Earth with an understated, droning E9sus4 chord, again hinting at an E Mixolydian tonality. The harmony is made even more interesting when heard against Redding's chromatically-tinged ascending bass line.

Fig. 50

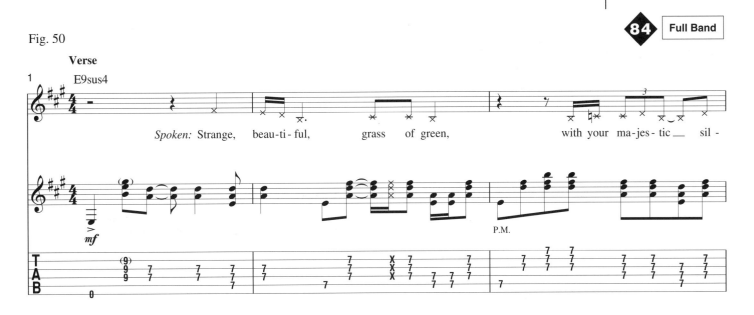

Spoken: Strange, beau-ti-ful, grass of green, with your ma-jes-tic sil-

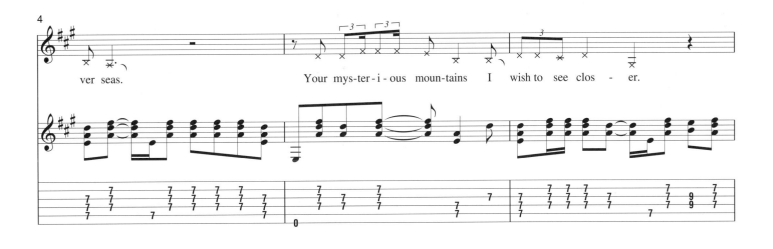

ver seas. Your mys-ter-i-ous moun-tains I wish to see clos-er.

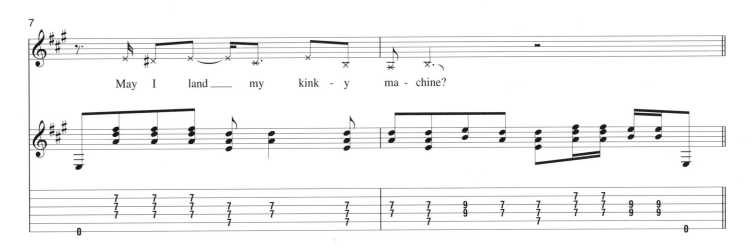

May I land my kink-y ma-chine?

Guitar Notation Legend

Guitar Music can be notated three different ways: on a *musical staff*, in *tablature*, and in *rhythm slashes*.

RHYTHM SLASHES are written above the staff. Strum chords in the rhythm indicated. Use the chord diagrams found at the top of the first page of the transcription for the appropriate chord voicings. Round noteheads indicate single notes.

THE MUSICAL STAFF shows pitches and rhythms and is divided by bar lines into measures. Pitches are named after the first seven letters of the alphabet.

TABLATURE graphically represents the guitar fingerboard. Each horizontal line represents a a string, and each number represents a fret.

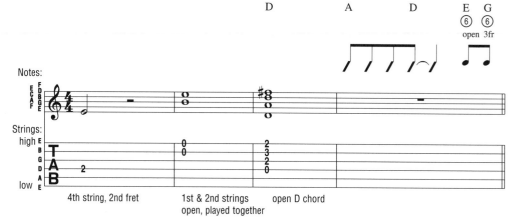

4th string, 2nd fret

1st & 2nd strings open, played together

open D chord

Definitions for Special Guitar Notation

HALF-STEP BEND: Strike the note and bend up 1/2 step.

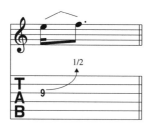

WHOLE-STEP BEND: Strike the note and bend up one step.

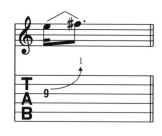

GRACE NOTE BEND: Strike the note and immediately bend up as indicated.

SLIGHT (MICROTONE) BEND: Strike the note and bend up 1/4 step.

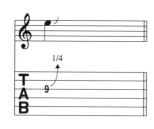

BEND AND RELEASE: Strike the note and bend up as indicated, then release back to the original note. Only the first note is struck.

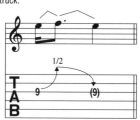

PRE-BEND: Bend the note as indicated, then strike it.

PRE-BEND AND RELEASE: Bend the note as indicated. Strike it and release the bend back to the original note.

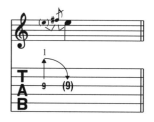

UNISON BEND: Strike the two notes simultaneously and bend the lower note up to the pitch of the higher.

VIBRATO: The string is vibrated by rapidly bending and releasing the note with the fretting hand.

WIDE VIBRATO: The pitch is varied to a greater degree by vibrating with the fretting hand.

HAMMER-ON: Strike the first (lower) note with one finger, then sound the higher note (on the same string) with another finger by fretting it without picking.

PULL-OFF: Place both fingers on the notes to be sounded. Strike the first note and without picking, pull the finger off to sound the second (lower) note.

LEGATO SLIDE: Strike the first note and then slide the same fret-hand finger up or down to the second note. The second note is not struck.

SHIFT SLIDE: Same as legato slide, except the second note is struck.

TRILL: Very rapidly alternate between the notes indicated by continuously hammering on and pulling off.

TAPPING: Hammer ("tap") the fret indicated with the pick-hand index or middle finger and pull off to the note fretted by the fret hand.

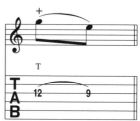

NATURAL HARMONIC: Strike the note while the fret-hand lightly touches the string directly over the fret indicated.

PINCH HARMONIC: The note is fretted normally and a harmonic is produced by adding the edge of the thumb or the tip of the index finger of the pick hand to the normal pick attack.

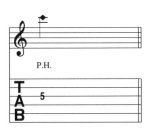

HARP HARMONIC: The note is fretted normally and a harmonic is produced by gently resting the pick hand's index finger directly above the indicated fret (in parentheses) while the pick hand's thumb or pick assists by plucking the appropriate string.

PICK SCRAPE: The edge of the pick is rubbed down (or up) the string, producing a scratchy sound.

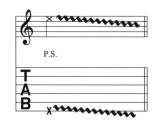

MUFFLED STRINGS: A percussive sound is produced by laying the fret hand across the string(s) without depressing, and striking them with the pick hand.

PALM MUTING: The note is partially muted by the pick hand lightly touching the string(s) just before the bridge.

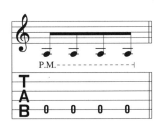

RAKE: Drag the pick across the strings indicated with a single motion.

TREMOLO PICKING: The note is picked as rapidly and continuously as possible.

ARPEGGIATE: Play the notes of the chord indicated by quickly rolling them from bottom to top.

VIBRATO BAR DIVE AND RETURN: The pitch of the note or chord is dropped a specified number of steps (in rhythm) then returned to the original pitch.

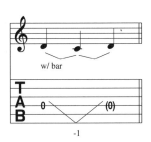

VIBRATO BAR SCOOP: Depress the bar just before striking the note, then quickly release the bar.

VIBRATO BAR DIP: Strike the note and then immediately drop a specified number of steps, then release back to the original pitch.

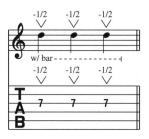

Additional Musical Definitions

(accent)	• Accentuate note (play it louder)	
(accent)	• Accentuate note with great intensity	
(staccato)	• Play the note short	
	• Downstroke	
∨	• Upstroke	

Rhy. Fig.	• Label used to recall a recurring accompaniment pattern (usually chordal).
Riff	• Label used to recall composed, melodic lines (usually single notes) which recur.
Fill	• Label used to identify a brief melodic figure which is to be inserted into the arrangement.
Rhy. Fill	• A chordal version of a Fill.
tacet	• Instrument is silent (drops out).

D.S. al Coda — • Go back to the sign (𝄋), then play until the measure marked "**To Coda**," then skip to the section labelled "**Coda**."

D.C. al Fine — • Go back to the beginning of the song and play until the measure marked "**Fine**" (end).

• Repeat measures between signs.

• When a repeated section has different endings, play the first ending only the first time and the second ending only the second time.

NOTE: Tablature numbers in parentheses mean:
1. The note is being sustained over a system (note in standard notation is tied), or
2. The note is sustained, but a new articulation (such as a hammer-on, pull-off, slide or vibrato begins), or
3. The note is a barely audible "ghost" note (note in standard notation is also in parentheses).

GUITAR *signature licks*®

Signature Licks book/CD packs provide a step-by-step breakdown of "right from the record" riffs, licks, and solos so you can jam along with your favorite bands. They contain performance notes and an overview of each artist's or group's style, with note-for-note transcriptions in notes and tab. The CDs feature full-band demos at both normal and slow speeds.

BEST OF ACOUSTIC GUITAR
00695640 ....$19.95

AEROSMITH 1973-1979
00695106 ....$22.95

AEROSMITH 1979-1998
00695219 ....$22.95

BEST OF AGGRO-METAL
00695592 ....$19.95

BEST OF CHET ATKINS
00695752 ....$22.95

THE BEACH BOYS DEFINITIVE COLLECTION
00695683 ....$22.95

BEST OF THE BEATLES FOR ACOUSTIC GUITAR
00695453 ....$22.95

THE BEATLES BASS
00695283 ....$22.95

THE BEATLES FAVORITES
00695096 ....$24.95

THE BEATLES HITS
00695049 ....$24.95

BEST OF GEORGE BENSON
00695418 ....$22.95

BEST OF BLACK SABBATH
00695249 ....$22.95

BEST OF BLINK 182
00695704 ....$22.95

BEST OF BLUES GUITAR
00695846 ....$19.95

BLUES GUITAR CLASSICS
00695177 ....$19.95

BLUES/ROCK GUITAR MASTERS
00695348 ....$19.95

BEST OF CHARLIE CHRISTIAN
00695584 ....$22.95

BEST OF ERIC CLAPTON
00695038 ....$24.95

ERIC CLAPTON – THE BLUESMAN
00695040 ....$22.95

ERIC CLAPTON – FROM THE ALBUM UNPLUGGED
00695250 ....$24.95

BEST OF CREAM
00695251 ....$22.95

DEEP PURPLE – GREATEST HITS
00695625 ....$22.95

THE DOORS
00695373 ....$22.95

FAMOUS ROCK GUITAR SOLOS
00695590 ....$19.95

BEST OF FOO FIGHTERS
00695481 ....$22.95

GREATEST GUITAR SOLOS OF ALL TIME
00695301 ....$19.95

BEST OF GRANT GREEN
00695747 ....$22.95

GUITAR INSTRUMENTAL HITS
00695309 ....$19.95

GUITAR RIFFS OF THE '60S
00695218 ....$19.95

BEST OF GUNS N' ROSES
00695183 ....$22.95

HARD ROCK SOLOS
00695591 ....$19.95

JIMI HENDRIX
00696560 ....$24.95

HOT COUNTRY GUITAR
00695580 ....$19.95

BEST OF JAZZ GUITAR
00695586 ....$24.95

ERIC JOHNSON
00699317 ....$22.95

ROBERT JOHNSON
00695264 ....$22.95

THE ESSENTIAL ALBERT KING
00695713 ....$22.95

B.B. KING – THE DEFINITIVE COLLECTION
00695635 ....$22.95

THE KINKS
00695553 ....$22.95

BEST OF KISS
00699413 ....$22.95

MARK KNOPFLER
00695178 ....$22.95

BEST OF YNGWIE MALMSTEEN
00695669 ....$22.95

BEST OF PAT MARTINO
00695632 ....$22.95

MEGADETH
00695041 ....$22.95

WES MONTGOMERY
00695387 ....$22.95

BEST OF NIRVANA
00695483 ....$24.95

THE OFFSPRING
00695852 ....$24.95

VERY BEST OF OZZY OSBOURNE
00695431 ....$22.95

BEST OF JOE PASS
00695730 ....$22.95

PINK FLOYD – EARLY CLASSICS
00695566 ....$22.95

THE POLICE
00695724 ....$22.95

THE GUITARS OF ELVIS
00696507 ....$22.95

BEST OF QUEEN
00695097 ....$22.95

BEST OF RAGE AGAINST THE MACHINE
00695480 ....$22.95

RED HOT CHILI PEPPERS
00695173 ....$22.95

RED HOT CHILI PEPPERS – GREATEST HITS
00695828 ....$24.95

BEST OF DJANGO REINHARDT
00695660 ....$22.95

BEST OF ROCK 'N' ROLL GUITAR
00695559 ....$19.95

BEST OF ROCKABILLY GUITAR
00695785 ....$19.95

THE ROLLING STONES
00695079 ....$22.95

BEST OF JOE SATRIANI
00695216 ....$22.95

BEST OF SILVERCHAIR
00695488 ....$22.95

BEST OF SOUTHERN ROCK
00695560 ....$19.95

ROD STEWART
00695663 ....$22.95

BEST OF SYSTEM OF A DOWN
00695788 ....$22.95

STEVE VAI
00673247 ....$22.95

STEVE VAI – ALIEN LOVE SECRETS: THE NAKED VAMPS
00695223 ....$22.95

STEVE VAI – FIRE GARDEN: THE NAKED VAMPS
00695166 ....$22.95

STEVE VAI – THE ULTRA ZONE: NAKED VAMPS
00695684 ....$22.95

STEVIE RAY VAUGHAN
00699316 ....$24.95

THE GUITAR STYLE OF STEVIE RAY VAUGHAN
00695155 ....$24.95

BEST OF THE VENTURES
00695772 ....$19.95

THE WHO
00695561 ....$22.95

BEST OF ZZ TOP
00695738 ....$22.95

Complete descriptions and songlists online!

FOR MORE INFORMATION, SEE YOUR LOCAL MUSIC DEALER, OR WRITE TO:

HAL•LEONARD® CORPORATION
7777 W. BLUEMOUND RD. P.O. BOX 13819 MILWAUKEE, WI 53213

www.halleonard.com

Prices, contents and availability subject to change without notice.

Get Better At Guitar

...with These Great Guitar Instruction Books from Hal Leonard!

101 GUITAR TIPS

INCLUDES TAB

STUFF ALL THE PROS KNOW AND USE

by Adam St. James

This book contains invaluable guidance on everything from scales and music theory to truss rod adjustments, proper recording studio set-ups, and much more. The book also features snippets of advice from some of the most celebrated guitarists and producers in the music business, including B.B. King, Steve Vai, Joe Satriani, Warren Haynes, Laurence Juber, Pete Anderson, Tom Dowd and others, culled from the author's hundreds of interviews.

_____00695737 Book/CD Pack $14.95

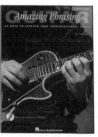

AMAZING PHRASING

INCLUDES TAB

50 WAYS TO IMPROVE YOUR IMPROVISATIONAL SKILLS

by Tom Kolb

This book/CD pack explores all the main components necessary for crafting well-balanced rhythmic and melodic phrases. It also explains how these phrases are put together to form cohesive solos. Many styles are covered – rock, blues, jazz, fusion, country, Latin, funk and more – and all of the concepts are backed up with musical examples. The companion CD contains 89 demos for listening, and most tracks feature full-band backing.

_____00695583 Book/CD Pack $16.95

BARRE CHORDS

AN EASY INTRODUCTION TO MOVEABLE FRETBOARD SHAPES

by Adam Perlmutter

Learn to master any chord progression, anywhere on the guitar! With just a few different chord shapes, you can strum through hundreds of songs – from blues to rock to folk and beyond. Includes: famous progressions from hit songs in all styles • notes & tab • barre chords in alternate tunings • and more. Learn riffs from artists such as: James Brown, Eric Clapton, Nirvana, The Police, Soundgarden, The Who and others.

_____00695746 Book/CD Pack $14.95

BLUES YOU CAN USE

INCLUDES TAB

by John Ganapes

A comprehensive source designed to help guitarists develop both lead and rhythm playing. Covers: Texas, Delta, R&B, early rock and roll, gospel, blues/rock and more. Includes: 21 complete solos • chord progressions and riffs • turnarounds • moveable scales and more. CD features leads and full band backing.

_____00695007 Book/CD Pack $19.95

GUITAR DIAL 9-1-1

INCLUDES TAB

50 WAYS TO IMPROVE YOUR PLAYING ... NOW!!

by Ken Parille

Need to breathe new life into your guitar playing? This book is your admission into the Guitar ER! You'll learn to: expand your harmonic vocabulary • improvise with chromatic notes • create rhythmic diversity • improve your agility through helpful drills • supply soulful fills • create melodic lines through chord changes • and much more! The accompanying CD includes 99 demonstration tracks.

_____00695405 Book/CD Pack $16.95

THE GUITAR F/X COOKBOOK

INCLUDES TAB

by Chris Amelar

The ultimate source for guitar tricks, effects, and other unorthodox techniques. This book demonstrates and explains 45 incredible guitar sounds using common stomp boxes and a few unique techniques, including: pick scraping, police siren, ghost slide, church bell, jaw harp, delay swells, looping, monkey's scream, cat's meow, race car, pickup tapping, and much more.

_____00695080 Book/CD Pack $14.95

GUITAR TECHNIQUES

INCLUDES TAB

by Michael Mueller

Guitar Techniques is a terrific reference and teaching companion, as it clearly defines and demonstrates how to properly execute cool moves ranging from bending, vibrato and legato to tapping, whammy bar and playing with your teeth! The CD contains 92 demonstration tracks in country, rock, pop and jazz styles. Essential techniques covered include: fretting • strumming • trills • picking • vibrato • tapping • bends • harmonics • muting • slides • and more.

_____00695562 Book/CD Pack $14.95

THE GUITARIST'S SURVIVAL KIT

INCLUDES TAB

EVERYTHING YOU NEED TO KNOW TO BE A WORKING MUSICIAN

by Dale Turner

From repertoire to accompaniment patterns to licks, this book is fully stocked to give you the confidence knowing you can "get by" and survive, regardless of the situation. The book covers: songs and set lists • gear • rhythm riffs in styles from blues to funk to rock to metal • lead licks in blues, country, jazz & rock styles • transposition and more. The CD features 99 demonstration tracks, and the book includes standard notation and tab.

_____00695380 Book/CD Pack $14.95

PICTURE CHORD ENCYCLOPEDIA

The most comprehensive guitar chord resource ever begins with helpful notes on how to use the book, how to choose the best voicings and how to construct chords. This extensive 272-page source for all playing styles and levels features five easy-to-play voicings of 44 chord qualities for each of the twelve musical keys – 2,640 chords in all! For each, there is a clearly illustrated chord frame, as well as *an actual photo* of the chord being played! Includes info on basic fingering principles, open chords and barre chords, partial chords and broken-set forms, and more. Great for all guitarists!

_____00695224 ....$19.95

POWER CHORDS

INCLUDES TAB

A COMPLETE GUIDE TO ROCK'S MOST ESSENTIAL SOUND

by Adam Perlmutter

Learn to master rock's most tried-and-true sound: the power chord. With just a few different power chord shapes, you can rock through hundreds of songs – from death metal, to rockabilly, to grunge and beyond. This book/CD pack includes: famous progressions from popular songs, by artists from Alice in Chains to Weezer • clear photos and frames of all the essential power chords • riffs in all styles • alternate tunings • notes and tab.

_____00695745 Book/CD Pack $14.95

SCALE CHORD RELATIONSHIPS

INCLUDES TAB

by Michael Mueller & Jeff Schroedl

Scale Chord Relationships teaches players how to determine which scales to play with which chords, so guitarists will never have to fear chord changes again! This book/CD pack explains how to: recognize keys • analyze chord progressions • use the modes • play over nondiatonic harmony • use harmonic and melodic minor scales • use symmetrical scales such as chromatic, whole-tone and diminished scales • incorporate exotic scales such as Hungarian major and Gypsy minor • and much more!

_____00695563 Book/CD Pack $14.95

TOTAL ROCK GUITAR

INCLUDES TAB

A COMPLETE GUIDE TO LEARNING ROCK GUITAR

by Troy Stetina

Total Rock Guitar is a unique and comprehensive source for learning rock guitar, designed to develop both lead and rhythm playing. This book/CD pack covers: getting a tone that rocks • open chords, power chords and barre chords • riffs, scales and licks • string bending, strumming, palm muting, harmonics and alternate picking • all rock styles • and much more. The examples in the book are in standard notation with chord grids and tablature, and the CD includes full-band backing for all 22 songs.

_____00695246 Book/CD Pack $17.95

RECORDED VERSIONS

The Best Note-For-Note Transcriptions Available

ALL BOOKS INCLUDE TABLATURE

00690501 Adams, Bryan – Greatest Hits $19.95	00690271 Johnson, Robert – New Transcriptions . . .$24.95	00690511 Reinhardt, Django – Definitive Collection . .$19.95
00692015 Aerosmith – Greatest Hits $22.95	00699131 Joplin, Janis – Best of $19.95	00690643 Relient K – Two Lefts Don't
00690178 Alice in Chains – Acoustic $19.95	00690651 Juanes – Exitos de Juanes $19.95	Make a Right...But Three Do $19.95
00690387 Alice in Chains – Nothing Safe:	00690427 Judas Priest – Best of $19.95	00690631 Rolling Stones – Guitar Anthology $24.95
The Best of the Box $19.95	00690742 Killers, The – Hot Fuss $19.95	00690685 Roth, David Lee – Eat 'Em and Smile $19.95
00694932 Allman Brothers Band – Volume 1 . . . . . .$24.95	00690444 King, B.B. and Eric Clapton –	00690694 Roth, David Lee – Guitar Anthology $24.95
00694933 Allman Brothers Band – Volume 2 . . . . . .$24.95	Riding with the King $19.95	00690749 Saliva – Survival of the Sickest $19.95
00690609 Audioslave $19.95	00690157 Kiss – Alive $19.95	00690031 Santana's Greatest Hits $19.95
00690366 Bad Company – Original Anthology, Book 1 . .$19.95	00694903 Kiss – Best of $24.95	00690566 Scorpions – Best of $19.95
00690503 Beach Boys – Very Best of $19.95	00690156 Kiss $17.95	00690659 Seger, Bob and the Silver Bullet Band –
00690489 Beatles – 1 . . . .$24.95	00690658 Lang, Johnny – Long Time Coming $19.95	Greatest Hits, Volume 2 . . . .$17.95
00694929 Beatles – 1962-1966 . . . .$24.95	00690614 Lavigne, Avril – Let Go $19.95	00690604 Seger, Bob – Guitar Collection $19.95
00694930 Beatles – 1967-1970 . . . .$24.95	00690726 Lavigne, Avril – Under My Skin $19.95	00690750 Shepherd, Kenny Wayne –
00694832 Beatles – For Acoustic Guitar $22.95	00690743 Los Lonely Boys $19.95	The Place You're In $19.95
00690482 Beatles – Let It Be $16.95	00690720 Lostprophets – Start Something $19.95	00690419 Slipknot $19.95
00690632 Beck – Sea Change $19.95	00690525 Lynch, George – Best of $19.95	00690530 Slipknot – Iowa $19.95
00692385 Berry, Chuck $19.95	00690577 Malmsteen, Yngwie – Anthology $24.95	00690733 Slipknot – Vol. 3 (The Subliminal Verses) . .$19.95
00692200 Black Sabbath –	00694956 Marley, Bob – Legend $19.95	00120004 Steely Dan – Best of $24.95
We Sold Our Soul for Rock 'N' Roll $19.95	00690548 Marley, Bob – One Love: Very Best of $19.95	00694921 Steppenwolf – Best of $22.95
00690674 Blink-182 . . . .$19.95	00694945 Marley, Bob – Songs of Freedom $24.95	00690689 Story of the Year – Page Avenue $19.95
00690389 Blink-182 – Enema of the State $19.95	00690748 Maroon5 – 1.22.03 Acoustic $19.95	00690520 Styx Guitar Collection $19.95
00690523 Blink-182 – Take Off Your Pants & Jacket . .$19.95	00690657 Maroon5 – Songs About Jane $19.95	00120081 Sublime $19.95
00690008 Bon Jovi – Cross Road $19.95	00690616 Matchbox 20 – More Than You Think You Are . .$19.95	00690519 Sum 41 – All Killer No Filler $19.95
00690491 Bowie, David – Best of $19.95	00690239 Matchbox 20 – Yourself or Someone Like You . .$19.95	00690612 Sum 41 – Does This Look Infected? $19.95
00690451 Buckley, Jeff – Collection $24.95	00690382 McLachlan, Sarah – Mirrorball $19.95	00690606 System of a Down – Steal This Album $19.95
00690590 Clapton, Eric – Anthology $29.95	00120080 McLean, Don – Songbook $19.95	00690531 System of a Down – Toxicity $19.95
00692391 Clapton, Eric – Best of, 2nd Edition $22.95	00694952 Megadeth – Countdown to Extinction $19.95	00694824 Taylor, James – Best of $16.95
00690415 Clapton Chronicles – Best of Eric Clapton . .$18.95	00694951 Megadeth – Rust in Peace $22.95	00694887 Thin Lizzy – Best of $19.95
00690074 Clapton, Eric – The Cream of Clapton $24.95	00690505 Mellencamp, John – Guitar Collection . . .$19.95	00690238 Third Eye Blind $19.95
00690716 Clapton, Eric – Me and Mr. Johnson $19.95	00690562 Metheny, Pat – Bright Size Life $19.95	00690738 3 Doors Down – Away from the Sun $22.95
00694869 Clapton, Eric – Unplugged $22.95	00690559 Metheny, Pat – Question and Answer $19.95	00690737 3 Doors Down – The Better Life $22.95
00690162 Clash – Best of The $19.95	00690565 Metheny, Pat – Rejoicing $19.95	00690665 Thursday – War All the Time $19.95
00690682 Coldplay – Live 2003 . . . .$19.95	00690040 Miller, Steve, Band – Young Hearts $19.95	00690654 Train – Best of $19.95
00690494 Coldplay – Parachutes $19.95	00690103 Morissette, Alanis – Jagged Little Pill $19.95	00690683 Trower, Robin – Bridge of Sighs $19.95
00690593 Coldplay – A Rush of Blood to the Head . .$19.95	00690722 New Found Glory – Catalyst $19.95	00699191 U2 – Best of: 1980-1990 . . . .$19.95
00694940 Counting Crows – August & Everything After . .$19.95	00690611 Nirvana $22.95	00690732 U2 – Best of: 1990-2000 . . . .$19.95
00690401 Creed – Human Clay $19.95	00690189 Nirvana – From the Muddy	00690039 Vai, Steve – Alien Love Secrets $24.95
00690352 Creed – My Own Prison $19.95	Banks of the Wishkah $19.95	00690392 Vai, Steve – The Ultra Zone $19.95
00690551 Creed – Weathered $19.95	00694913 Nirvana – In Utero $19.95	00690370 Vaughan, Stevie Ray and Double Trouble –
00699521 Cure, The – Greatest Hits $24.95	00694883 Nirvana – Nevermind $19.95	The Real Deal: Greatest Hits Volume 2 . .$22.95
00690637 Dale, Dick – Best of $19.95	00690026 Nirvana – Unplugged in New York $19.95	00690116 Vaughan, Stevie Ray – Guitar Collection . . .$24.95
00690289 Deep Purple – Best of $17.95	00690739 No Doubt – Rock Steady $22.95	00660058 Vaughan, Stevie Ray –
00690384 Di Franco, Ani – Best of $19.95	00120112 No Doubt – Tragic Kingdom $22.95	Lightnin' Blues 1983-1987 . . . .$24.95
00690347 Doors, The – Anthology $22.95	00690358 Offspring, The – Americana $19.95	00694835 Vaughan, Stevie Ray – The Sky Is Crying . .$22.95
00690348 Doors, The – Essential Guitar Collection . .$16.95	00690663 Offspring, The – Splinter $19.95	00690015 Vaughan, Stevie Ray – Texas Flood $19.95
00690235 Foo Fighters – The Colour and the Shape . .$19.95	00694847 Osbourne, Ozzy – Best of $22.95	00694789 Waters, Muddy – Deep Blues $24.95
00690595 Foo Fighters – One by One $19.95	00690399 Osbourne, Ozzy – Ozzman Cometh $19.95	00690071 Weezer (The Blue Album) $19.95
00690734 Franz Ferdinand $19.95	00690594 Paul, Les – Best of $19.95	00690516 Weezer (The Green Album) $19.95
00690222 G3 Live – Satriani, Vai, Johnson $22.95	00694855 Pearl Jam – Ten $19.95	00690447 Who, The – Best of $24.95
00120167 Godsmack $19.95	00690439 Perfect Circle, A – Mer De Noms $19.95	00690596 Yardbirds, The – Best of $19.95
00690338 Goo Goo Dolls – Dizzy Up the Girl $19.95	00690661 Perfect Circle, A – Thirteenth Step $19.95	00690696 Yeah Yeah Yeahs – Fever to Tell $19.95
00690601 Good Charlotte –	00690499 Petty, Tom – The Definitive	00690710 Yellowcard – Ocean Avenue $19.95
The Young and the Hopeless $19.95	Guitar Collection $19.95	00690443 Zappa, Frank – Hot Rats $19.95
00690591 Griffin, Patty – Guitar Collection $19.95	00690240 Phish – Hoist $19.95	00690589 ZZ Top Guitar Anthology $22.95
00694798 Harrison, George – Anthology $19.95	00690731 Pillar – Where Do We Go from Here? $19.95	
00692930 Hendrix, Jimi – Are You Experienced? . . .$24.95	00690428 Pink Floyd – Dark Side of the Moon $19.95	
00692931 Hendrix, Jimi – Axis: Bold As Love $22.95	00693864 Police, The – Best of $19.95	
00690017 Hendrix, Jimi – Live at Woodstock $24.95	00694975 Queen – Greatest Hits $24.95	
00690602 Hendrix, Jimi – Smash Hits $19.95	00690670 Queensryche – Very Best of $19.95	
00690688 Incubus – A Crow Left of the Murder $19.95	00694910 Rage Against the Machine $19.95	
00690457 Incubus – Make Yourself $19.95	00690055 Red Hot Chili Peppers –	
00690544 Incubus – Morningview $19.95	Bloodsugarsexmagik $19.95	
00690652 Jane's Addiction – Best of $19.95	00690584 Red Hot Chili Peppers – By the Way $19.95	
00690721 Jet – Get Born $19.95	00690379 Red Hot Chili Peppers – Californication . .$19.95	
00690751 John5 – Vertigo $19.95	00690673 Red Hot Chili Peppers – Greatest Hits . . .$19.95	
00690660 Johnson, Eric – Best of $19.95